Surviving in Biafra

The Story of the Nigerian Civil War

Over two million died

Alfred Obiora Uzokwe, P.E.

Writers Advantage
New York Lincoln Shanghai

Surviving in Biafra
The Story of the Nigerian Civil War

Writers Advantage
an imprint of iUniverse, Inc.

For information address:
iUniverse
2021 Pine Lake Road, Suite 100
Lincoln, NE 68512
www.iuniverse.com

ISBN: 0-595-26366-6 (Pbk)
ISBN: 0-595-65586-6 (Cloth)

Printed in the United States of America

This book is dedicated to my brother, Captain Fidelis Ikechukwuka Uzokwe

ACKNOWLEDGEMENTS

My sincere thanks to my brother Nnamdi, for his unflinching support and continued insistence on quality for this project. His encouragement ensured the timely completion of the manuscript.

Special thanks to my children, Alfred Jr., Lilian, Sylvanus, Jenny and Chris, for reviewing the manuscript with me and giving their comments. Thanks to Alfred Jr. for taking the author picture on the back cover of this book.

Many thanks to my wife, Anthonia, for picking up the slack in the house as I worked to complete the manuscript. Ifeyinwa, your hard work is very much appreciated.

And to my mother, Mrs Lilian Uzokwe, who taught me the essence of perseverance, I say thank you, mama.

I thank Dr. Patrick Ukata, Esq., and Ana Marrie for diligently reviewing the manuscript and providing very valuable comments.

To Mr. Chuck Odili, the founder of Nigeriaworld.com, I say thanks for providing the forum in which the book project was born.

Thanks to my siblings, Ijeoma, Emma, Uche, Edith, Nnamdi and Chukwunonso, for their support as I told the story of our lives.

Many thanks to Sam Ojukwu of VOBR for the songs and Dawodu.com for the selected speeches published herein.

Thanks to my father, Sylvanus Chukwukadibia Uzokwe, posthumously, for his insistence on excellence in spoken and written English. Papa, although

I could not keep up with the Latin quips, I do hereby say to you, *Dominus vobiscum.*

Alfred Obiora Chukwukadibia Uzokwe, P.E.
December 2002.

CONTENTS

FOREWORD

By
Dr. Patrick Ukata, Esq.

It is for me both an honor and a privilege to have been asked by Alfred to write the foreword to *Surviving in Biafra*. This is a very well written book with informative illustrations where necessary. It captures the very essence of the series of crises that took place in Nigeria from 1966 to 1970, and includes information on what it was like to be a person from the Eastern part of Nigeria in the period leading to the civil war and during the war itself. Alfred presents a candid and very personal account of his experiences during this period.

Written from the point of view of a six-year-old experiencing these events, this book is very unique in that, to my knowledge, it is the first such portrayal of this conflict from that perspective. Other books that have been written on the subject have either been by the principal combatant actors themselves or by interested bystanders. In this book, Alfred tells the story of the, before now, voiceless people who lived in the then Republic of Biafra. This is so because, in effect, the book finally gives a voice to the many ordinary children and adults in Biafra who were only known due to the fact that their faces were continually plastered in newspapers all over the world during the civil war. In *Surviving in Biafra*, Alfred provides a captivating account of what it was like to be one of those children whose faces made the front pages of international newspapers. Also, as a survivior of Biafra myself, reading the book was like taking a walk down memory lane.

To those who may question the utility of writing this book about the civil war more than thirty-two years after the fact, I say to them, if not now, when? In my view, this book is certainly not an effort at revisionist history; rather, it makes a very valuable contribution to Nigerian history and politics. A survey of contemporary Nigerian history and politics suggests that

Nigerians have not learnt any lessons from the past. Events taking place today in Nigeria are sadly very reminiscent of similar occurrences that precipitated the secession of Biafra and the civil war. Presently, there is a heightened sense of insecurity and intolerance within Nigeria. Incidents of political and religiously motivated killings are occurring with alarming frequency. Many sections of Nigeria feel neglected and marginalized today just as they did before the civil war. In a way, it is as though history is repeating itself all over again. Therefore, a book like *Surviving in Biafra* is very necessary to help Nigerians to clearly understand the dangers inherent in not doing everything possible to ensure a peaceful coexistence among the multiplicity of ethnic groups that make up Nigeria. The book captures the painful memories of the millions of deaths associated with the civil war. It also documents the displacement of millions of others who became refugees during the war and the hardships they endured. I have the strong belief that no well-meaning Nigerian, or any other person for that matter, could read this book and fail to understand the human and material cost of intolerance. One of the book's many important contributions is that some of the events recounted in it serve as a somber reminder of what can happen when incidents of targeted killings, insecurity and intimidation go unchecked. Therefore, *Surviving in Biafra* is a must-read book for all those who would like to see Nigeria remain a peaceful political entity.

INTRODUCTION

Nigeria is situated in the western part of Africa and currently has a population of about 120 million. It consists of many ethnic groups, which speak more than 250 different dialects, but the central medium of communication is English.

There are three major ethnic groups in the country: the Hausas, who primarily inhabit the northern region of Nigeria, the Yorubas in the western region and the Igbo people in the eastern region.

Map of Africa
showing the location
of Nigeria on the
western part.

Prior to the year 1914, these three distinct groups and other ethnic groups were leading their lives independent of one another. The British colonial masters, in what was called the Amalgamation of Northern and Southern Protectorates, brought them all together into one single unit called Nigeria. The colonialists drew artificial boundaries which did not consider cultural incongruity that existed between the people they were herding together. The boundaries were drawn to make it easy for them to administer the new nation they had created. Naturally, this amalgamation of people with diverse social, political, cultural and ideological inclinations brought about inter-ethnic squabbles and religious conflicts in the nation. The people of the northern region (the Hausas) were mainly Muslims, while those of the southern region were mainly Christians. Forced to live together in one nation through the amalgamation, the people of Nigeria learnt to coexist side by side while a cold war continued to brew by way of ethnic tensions.

During the struggle for Nigeria's Independence from Britain, which intensified in the 1950s, the various ethnic groups worked together. It is conceivable that because they had a common goal of liberation from their colonial masters, their differences seemed to be submerged by their larger goal of independence. In 1960, Nigeria gained independence from Britain. Naturally, the differences that had always existed in their ways of life, culture and ideology, resurfaced. This led to a series of disturbances, culminating in a chain of uprisings and military coups. During these uprisings, the ethnic groups were pitted against one another and many people were massacred in cold blood. The last straw that broke the camel's back was the riots of 1966, in which thousands of people from the eastern region, who were living in the northern region, were massacred in cold blood by their northern Nigerian counterparts. The killings convinced the easterners that their safety could no longer be guaranteed outside of the eastern region, and so a mass exodus of easterners from the northern states ensued. The easterners left the northern and western regions in droves and fled back to their native eastern region.

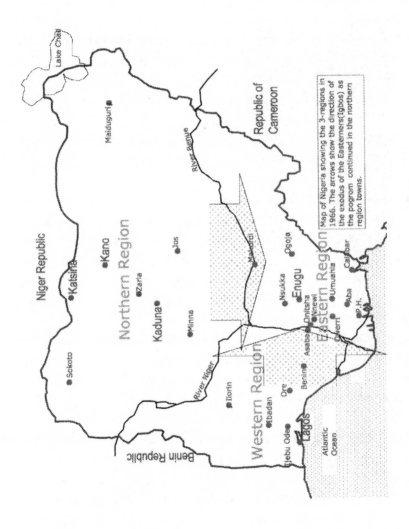

Finally, with the mandate of the eastern region house of assembly, the then governor of Eastern Nigeria, who is also an Igbo, Col. Chukwuemeka

Odumegwu Ojukwu, on May 30, 1967, declared the secession of the eastern region from the nation of Nigeria. The new nation was called Biafra.

Refusing to accept the sovereignty of Biafra, the government of Nigeria, led by Col. Yakubu Gowon, declared the secession illegal and mobilized about 100,000 troops, mainly made up of people of Hausa and Yoruba ethnic origins, to fight the soldiers of the eastern region. The massive military offensive against Biafra was an attempt to reintegrate her into the Nigerian fold, Col. Yakubu Gowon later said. Refusing to be forced into a nation where their safety was now in question, Biafra took up arms in her defense, and hence a 30-month civil war between Nigeria and the new nation of Biafra started.

My family is from Nnewi, in eastern Nigeria. Before the war started, we were living in the capital of Nigeria, Lagos, but as hostilities against the easterners started, we were forced to leave Lagos and return to our hometown. This book is the story of what I saw as a little boy. It is in effect the story of survival in Biafra. There have been several accounts of the war authored by men who prosecuted the war or witnessed the events directly as they unfolded on the warfronts. They saw the war through the eyes of adults; some authors like Col. J.O.G Achuzia talked about their heroics in the war, while others, like General Madiebo, pointed out things they felt were inimical to the effective prosecution of the war on the Biafran side. Other authors, like Frederick Forsyth, characterized Biafra as an entity that would have risen to become a great nation had she survived.

My account on Biafra is not about heroic feats because I did not perform any. I was just seven when the war commenced and by the time it officially ended in 1970, I was a ten-year-old boy. This is very significant though; I spent three of my formative years in Biafra under siege by the Nigerian military troops. My account is therefore about survival in Biafra seen through the eyes of a kid; a kid who saw other kids die of hunger; a kid who witnessed the onslaught of air raids and their deadly effects; a kid who watched grieving families bury their sons and fathers prematurely. Hopefully, this book will provide an insight into what other kids felt which no one has ever reported or bothered to try reporting.

WHY I WROTE THIS BOOK

It troubles me immensely every time I hear people suggest that the unfortunate story of the Biafran war should not be told or discussed; they reason that since people are trying to put the experience behind them, further discussion would be tantamount to reopening old wounds. When I hear such ill-informed advice, I usually respond with the age-old saying that those who shy away from history are doomed to repeat it. At the end of that war, there should have been an honest and thorough assessment of what had happened as well as a review of the roles played by all participants. The result of the assessment should have been used as the basis to "design" a better Nigeria.

After the war, the Nigerian government was in such a hurry to lay every blame on the doorstep of the Igbos that it missed the opportunity for an After Action Review, which would have led to true reconciliation, reconstruction and rehabilitation. As a result, 33 years after the war, most of the problems that led to that tragic war still linger. Today in Nigeria, interethnic animosity, domination and suspicion still abound. Citizens are still calling for a national conference where all groups would sit round the table to determine the conditions for coexistence because they are not satisfied with the structure of the government. The military is still dominated by soldiers of northern Nigerian origin, fueling suspicion that the North wants to perpetually dominate the country. Killings, especially of Christians, generated by religious intolerance in the northern states, is still rife, and political violence is the order of the day. These were some of the problems that brought about the war of 1967 and as it stands today, they have not gone away.

It is with all this in mind that I decided to tell the story of Biafra. I want Nigerians to remember what happened during that war and to reflect on the suffering that civilians, women, children and the elderly had to bear. I want them to remember that the cost of that war, in terms of human lives and property, was enormous. I want the story of the Biafran war to be kept in the forefront of Nigeria's national discourse to help prevent a repeat of that tragic episode.

On the 7th of December 2001, the United States of America commemorated the 60th anniversary of the bombing of the Pearl Harbor by the Japanese. As painful as that experience was, America still chose to remember it. Why? They used the occasion to honor those who lost their lives in the defense of America. Also, remembrance of what happened on that fateful day helps ensure that measures are put in place to avoid a similar occurrance. This is the hallmark of an advanced and civilized society; you forgive, but do not forget. The Biafran war, which took the lives of over two million people, should not be an exception. The men, women and children who lost their lives as a result of that conflict must not be forgotten. The harrowing experience of those who survived the war must not be swept under the rug. It is the intent of this book to ensure that we do not forget the horrors of those days while marching ahead in the quest for the development and realization of a better Nigeria

1

Lagos, Nigeria, 1966

In 1966, I was just a six-year-old boy living with my family in Lagos, Nigeria. Even at that young age, I was very much aware of the political rumblings and disturbances in northern Nigeria. The issue seemed to dominate the radio airwaves and my parents always talked about the killing of Igbos in the North. It bothered my father that the nation was drifting aimlessly, and he always prognosticated that the killings, coupled with political instability in the nation, could degenerate into a full-blown war. In spite of all the depressing news, I saw life as normal because in my mind, political upheavals were part of normal occurrences in life. I loved Lagos a lot, not only because I had a lot of friends to play with, but also because of the modern conveniences there, like electricity, which I did not see when we had earlier visited my hometown. During that visit to Nnewi, it bothered me that once darkness fell, everywhere became pitch black, with an eerie silence enveloping the village like a vice. For lighting during dark hours, we used what we called tili *lamp*, or gas lamp, which was always turned off after 9:00 p.m. I dreaded getting up in the night even to relieve myself because the outhouse was located about 300 feet away from the main house. It did not help that very big trees surrounded our compound. Even though the trees gave the environment a very serene disposition during the daytime, at night it felt like the darkness was lying in wait to swallow the compound and its inhabitants at the slightest opportunity.

In Lagos, there was electricity. We had a refrigerator and it housed cold drinks and ice cream, which I enjoyed immensely. I also liked the fact that one could get instant hot water for showers on cool harmattan mornings

1

when cool, dry and dust-laden winds blow from the Sahara desert in North Africa, into Nigeria.

Another luxury we enjoyed in Lagos was movies. My father was the welfare officer at the Yaba College of Technology and so we lived in the staff quarters inside the campus grounds. With this came the privilege of joining the students of the college to watch occasional cinema (*silima*) shows in the college grounds. I loved those movies and I remember that every time an upcoming movie show was announced, I was usually filled with unbridled sense of anticipation and excitement.

The many ghost stories about Lagos scared me though. My sister Ijeoma told us the story of Bisi, a girl who died in Lagos. Several months later, someone spotted her around Obalende bus stop. Of course like any other lad of my age, I believed those stories. There were also stories of abductors, or *ndi nto* as they were called in Igbo. They were said to be in every part of Lagos looking for little kids to abduct and sell to people with diabolical disposition; these people then mummified the kids and used their lifeless bodies to make money. According to the story, the mummified body was placed in a glass coffin in a very private room. Every time the owner wanted money, he would go into the private room, recite some magical incantations and money would flow out from an opening made especially for that purpose on the side of the coffin! These were always very frightening stories and they became effective deterrents for the kids against venturing out unaccompanied. In my house, kids had instructions not to talk to or follow strangers and to always go out in groups.

This was the time of General Ironsi, the Nigerian military head of state. He came to power following the violent military coup of January 1966. It seemed like the general was always in the news then. Radio broadcasts would often begin, "The head of state and supreme commander in chief of the Nigerian armed forces, Major General Johnson Thomas Umunnakwe Aguiyi Ironsi..." I always wondered why the general had so many names, and it intrigued me even more that broadcasters seemed compelled to always call out all his names during radio broadcasts. All these added to the enigmatic and sometimes incredulous disposition that was associated with the name of the Nigerian supreme commander. One story went around amongst the kids that the general was invincible; there was this famous photograph of him as he was leaving the United Nations peacekeeping mission in the troubled Central African Republic of Congo, waving good-bye with one hand and clutching a small crocodile replica in the other hand. I believe he was standing on the step of an aircraft. Legend had it that the crocodile was alive; it was credited to have saved his life during the UN peacekeeping mission in Congo. We were told that the crocodile made him invincible and therefore no amount of bullets could harm him. The Igbo term for crocodile is *aguiyi*. It is therefore conceivable that the general merely used the crocodile replica as a symbol of his middle name. Given all these stories about Ironsi's invincibility, we were shocked beyond belief when it was reported that he had been killed in a coup staged by soldiers of Northern Nigerian origin. They were embittered by the January 1966 coup, in which many leaders of the northern states were killed. After this counter coup, Lt. Col. Yakubu Gowon, a northerner, emerged as the new Nigerian head of state.

As the situation in the country continued to deteriorate, both as a result of Ironsi's murder and the killing of Igbos in the North, I could no longer go to school on a daily basis. I was in kindergarten at the Ladi-Lak Institute, Yaba Lagos. Pa-Bukola, a friend of my father, who used to bring Bukola and me back from school, no longer showed up at our house. We later concluded that as tension heightened between the Igbos and Hausas and as hostilities against the Igbo people grew in the North, he decided to keep away to avoid being branded an Igbo-lover, since he was of the Yoruba extraction. This was also true of my father's army buddy, whom we knew as *Sajin Major*. I believe he was a Regimental Sergeant Major (RSM) in the Nigerian Army. He was a tall, dark and heavily accented Hausa man whom I thought was very pleasant by all standards. During Christmas celebrations, my father would send gifts to him, and during Moslem holidays, Sajin Major always reciprocated. As the pogroms and genocide in the

North continued to gather momentum, and as stories of clandestine and nocturnal abductions and killings of Igbos in Lagos and environs started, my father got wind of the fact that *Sajin Major* had suddenly become a turncoat and wanted to make him an abduction statistic!

At first, my father could not believe this and simply attributed it to the handiwork of rumormongers and people of their ilk. Later on, evidence got even stronger that *Sajin Major* was ready to implement his evil plan, but my father still chose to do nothing. My maternal cousin, Edith, later interceded and nightly hiding places were established for my father. He started alternating sleeping places; some days he would sleep in his office inside the compound of Yaba College of Technology and other days he would sleep in my cousin's place at Ebute Metta. I could never forget my father's office because, before I went into kindergarten at the Ladi-Lak Institute, I used to spend some of my days there, with my chalkboard (slate) writing my ABCs and 123s. The talkative child I was then, I never failed to say a word or two to the students coming to the office to discuss their welfare issues with my father.

One night, sometime before midnight, three stern-looking men came to our house and demanded to see my father. Prior to that episode, we had already rehearsed a standard response about my father's whereabouts should anyone come calling. My mother was to act and sound distraught while saying she had not seen him that evening. We were to do the same. The men got angry with my mother when she told them that my father had not returned that evening. Even though these men never came back to our house afterwards, this singular incident strengthened our conviction that my father was not safe in his own home. I found all these developments incredulous; *Sajin Major* was my father's friend, I thought, why would he want his blood spilled? As a child, it never occurred to me that the ethnic divisions and intolerance in Nigeria had become so deep that friends were willing to sacrifice friends on the altar of ethnic loyalty. Whether *Sajin Major* was guilty or not, his actions made him appear guilty. As those events unfolded, he never showed up in our house again. In my mind, if he had just made himself scarce when he felt that he could no longer be friends with my family because of ethnic tensions, it would have made more sense. It disturbed me that he was making efforts to shed the blood of someone who had never done anything wrong to him, someone who was his very good friend. From stories we later heard, many Igbo families who were killed in the North died directly or indirectly at the hands of their northern Nigerian friends and neighbors. Some were betrayed and delivered into the hands of mobs that were rampaging through the streets, burning down houses and human beings, hacking people to death and raping young girls.

All kinds of rumors pervaded the nation concerning the manner in which General Ironsi was killed; some said he was confronted by soldiers at the state house in Ibadan and shot. Others said he was tied to the back of a jeep and dragged along until his body decapitated. These were stories kids told one another. The issues were always discussed in hushed tones by adults, and I do know that the period in question must have been filled with bad news because every time my father read the newspaper, one could see sad expressions written all over his face.

This reminds me of when Sir Odumegwu Ojukwu, the father of the then governor of eastern Nigeria, died. This may have happened a year or so before 1966. My mother was listening to the radio and suddenly let out a loud shout of *ewo-o-o*. Without waiting to hear what happened, my sister Edith ran out of the house and before we knew it, my father was back in the house. Edith had told him that something really bad had happened at home and that my mother was crying. I could hear him asking my mother breathlessly, "What happened?" My mother explained that Sir Odumegwu Ojukwu had died. For some reason, I had never heard the name Sir Ojukwu before then, but I knew from the expression on the faces of my parents that a very important person had died. Little did I know then that the name Odumegwu Ojukwu would be a name I would subsequently hear on a daily basis between 1967 and 1970. This time it was to be the young

leader of the breakaway republic of Biafra, Lt. Colonel Chukwuemeka
Odumegwu Ojukwu.

Anyhow, I never realized the gravity and implication of what was
unfolding in Nigeria in those tumultuous days of 1966. I had accepted the
fact that I could not immediately go back to my school every weekday
because of safety concerns, but I was unprepared for what happened the
next time we went to Sunday school. Sunday school was always fun; a lot of
other Igbo children attended that church. After Sunday school, we would
play for a while before heading back to our respective homes; it was enjoy-
able.

There was something ominous about one particular Sunday. As I
walked into the church premises with Uchenna and Edith, the usual hustle
and bustle of activities was absent; the little girls who would normally be
playing *oga* and *suwe* were nowhere to be found. Even inside the church,
only a handful of children were present. At the end of the Sunday school
class, the Sunday school teacher told us that many families had either gone
back to the eastern region or were in hiding because of the uncertainties
engendered by the killing of the easterners in the northern region. He also
cited the increase in harassment of Igbos in Lagos and outlying areas as
another reason for the mass exodus. Then, as if he had not elicited the
desired reaction from us, in a slow but deliberate tone, he somberly added,
"Many more of the families in Lagos will be leaving for the East before the
next Sunday school class."

My siblings and I narrated what transpired in the church to my mother
when we got back home, and for the first time she expressed apprehension
about our continued stay in Lagos. She stated that she had told our father
to resign from Yaba College so we could all go back to the East, to Nnewi.
She said that some of our family friends and neighbors had already left: the
Ngwubes, the Ikems, and the Unegbus. Even Mr. Igwilo, the college
groundskeeper (students called him *Kekere*) from Oraifite, near Nnewi,
had left. That did it for me! I could not go to school regularly anymore for
safety reasons; Sunday school was no longer going to be fun because most

kids would have left Lagos by the next Sunday and now I had no friends left to play with. I knew I could never enjoy Lagos again, not with the Ikem family—Irene, Nwamu ("Boy," as we called him) and Jenny—gone. From then on, sheer misery set in. I was ready to go back to Nnewi. I had only visited there once, but figured that I would at least have relatives there to play with

To compound an already terrible situation and for safety reasons, in response to increased rumors of abductions of Igbos, our movement was restricted to just walking around our house. In fact there was a story that there were some Igbo people who pretended to be Yorubas when unknown persons accosted them. To verify their true identity, they were asked to pronounce "Obalende." The story had it that a true Yoruba would say "OBAL-ENDE" but an Igbo would for some reason pronounce it as "OBALANDE." It was said that when the Igbos failed to pronounce Obalende properly, they were taken away.

The kids in my family were very lonely in the College of Technology compound because most of our Igbo friends had left for the East. Even though we were warned to always stay in the house to avoid attracting attention to ourselves as easterners, Uchenna, Nnamdi and I undertook a trip outside our house that resulted in tragedy. Our next-door neighbor was a man called Mr. Ikem; he was the college bursar. We were very close to his family and played with his children. They had a swing at the back of their house, which we called *janglover*. Before the Ikem family traveled back to the East to escape hostilities, we used to gather there to play on the swing, and to pick and eat a fruit we called *ogogo*. On this day, Uchenna decided to take us there to play on the swing even though the Ikem family had gone. When we got there, she mounted the swing and started swinging back and forth while Nnamdi and I were busy playing. Apparently, the family did not leave with one of their dogs called *Brownie*. We were very familiar with this dog and used to play with it in the past, so when it came out, we were comfortable around it. It went very close to where Uchenna was on the swing and lay down. At this time, Uche moved the swing and the tip of her toe touched the dog. All hell broke loose! The dog jumped up, sunk its teeth into her clothes and dragged her down. In the twinkle of an eye, the dog started mauling her ferociously while making a type of noise I had never heard in my life. It was dragging her all over the ground and mauling her. At this time, my little brother ran into a small room behind the main house and closed the door. That room (boys quarter) used to be inhabited by a relative of the Ikems named Sylvester. I just climbed up one of the small trees close by and from there helplessly watched as the dog brutally assaulted Uchenna; it was frightening. Just by God's grace, Sylvester ran out when he heard the commotion and with the stump of a tree that he picked up from the ground he lashed out at the dog, hitting it on the side. It was only then that the dog let go of Uchenna and ran away. We were surprised by Sylvester's sudden appearance because all the while we thought he had left Lagos along with the Ikem family. Of course, Uchenna was bleeding; my parents were contacted and she was taken to Igbobi hospital where she received stitches. She also received injections, which according to my mother, was a precautionary step against rabies.

This incident did not go down well with my father; first, we had disobeyed him by going out when we should not have, and to compound things, no one knew we had left our house. Also, even though we were trying to avoid attracting attention to our presence in the college compound, the news of what happened made its round within the campus, much to the chagrin of my father. Meanwhile, Nigeria's problems were getting worse by the day.

The whole atmosphere in the nation was replete with fear; the stories coming from the North were exceedingly gruesome. It was said that during one of the riots in the North, a pregnant Igbo woman was disemboweled and the unborn baby removed and killed also! There were also stories about Igbo people who had their eyes gouged out just to ridicule them before killing them. Some were simply hacked to death with machetes. Our anxiety level took a critical turn when my father was told point blank that his safety could no longer be guaranteed at the Yaba College of Technology.

This became a double whammy; he no longer slept in the house at night because of *Sajin Major* and now his safety could no longer be guaranteed. Life became exceedingly unbearable. Of course, my parents were also irritable as a result of the tensions. Little things raised their ire. All these compounded our problems as kids.

We wanted to go back to our hometown, Nnewi, but my father was the obdurate type—he seemed to believe that we could wait things out in Lagos and that soon things would return to normalcy, a belief he later regretted! We were literally begging him to send us to Nnewi, out of harm's way.

2

My family Goes Home to Nnewi

My mother worked as a nurse for the Lagos City Council. She was stationed at the Surulere Health Center. Initially, there were many nurses and doctors of eastern Nigerian origin working for the center. They had a common cloakroom where nurses hung their aprons and doctors hung their coats. Of course, the doctors' coats bore their names. As the situation of things in the country continued to nose-dive into a state of chaos, my mother observed that each time she went to work, the doctors' coats and nurses' aprons were reducing in number; she was seeing less and less of coats and aprons belonging to the Igbo doctors and nurses. Her inquiries revealed that the Igbos had started going home to the East. They were not even resigning formally; this was to avoid tipping off anyone. Back home, we were still begging our father to take us back to our hometown.

One day, my mother went to Mushin market to buy foodstuff for the family, as she customarily did. She was in the company of a friend of hers who hailed from Calabar; she was also a nurse. At the market, they set out to do the shopping, and in the end they came to a spot where some women were selling fresh fish. My mother asked one of the hawkers how much her fish cost and the lady told her that it cost about one and nine. That was the way in which one shilling and nine pence was referred to in those days. In open markets in Nigeria, it is generally regarded as stupidity if one fails to haggle the prices of goods before buying. In that spirit, my mother asked her if she would sell for one and three, which meant one shilling and three pence. At this juncture, the lady reacted belligerently and started unleashing unprintable invectives on my mother. She was cursing her in a combination of Yoruba dialect and pidgin English, all jumbled together. My mother and her friend were befuddled by her reaction because they could not immediately tell why the lady was that upset. My mother felt that even if she had terribly undercut the value of her fish, it was no reason to react the way she was. All she needed to do was to tell her that she would not sell. The cause of her reaction was still a mystery to my mother as she stood there helplessly, until the woman said, "*No be your people them they butcher for north and you come here to buy fish for one and three? Go back to the East and see who go sell you fish for one and three.*" My mother was livid! It became obvious that the woman's reaction was born out of hate, not because my mother had undervalued her fish. At this juncture, the fighting spirit in my mother took over. Before she could leap forward to pounce on the woman, she was restrained by the Calabar lady, who whispered to her that they were outnumbered there and could actually be lynched in Mushin market by the small crowd that had now gathered to see what the commotion was all about. My mother took the wise counsel of the lady and they went home. After that day, she increased pressure on my father to take us all back to Nnewi. She felt that in the face of all the tragedy the Igbos were facing, here was a market woman rubbing it in with reckless abandon! My mother hated the insensitivity with which the lady said it to her; it betrayed the underlying ethnic intolerance that was sweeping across the nation like a pest-laden wind.

My father continued to dilly-dally about taking us home, but when the gory details of the massacre of Igbos in the North became overwhelming, he finally gave in to our requests to return to our hometown. Our departure date was set and we were instructed to "tell no one about it." The logistics for transporting all our belongings and our family to Nnewi became the next hurdle to leap. My family was a large one by all standards: there were four boys and three girls plus my parents. At the time though, my eldest brother, Fidelis, was away in secondary school at the Merchants of Light School, Oba, in the East. My other brother, Emmanuel, was at Ika Grammar School, Agbor, in the Midwest. Even in the absence of two of my brothers, we still had seven people plus our personal belongings to transport to Nnewi. My father's brand new Opel Cadet was a compact car that barely sat five people; to contemplate seating seven people and their belongings made no sense. The kids, however, did not worry about the seeming transportation problem; we felt that our parents would have it all worked out.

I had visited Nnewi only once in my life and even though I preferred staying in Lagos at that time, I still liked Nnewi because my grandmother and aunts pampered us a lot during the Christmas period, when we visited. I saw Nnewi as peaceful, bucolic and quaint, with trees ubiquitously scattered all over the place and birds chirping incessantly. I also remembered the Christmas masquerades called *opiakamkpala* and *ikedinodogwu*, which we saw during that visit. On Christmas Day, the masquerades made rounds, chasing kids from place to place; some danced from house to house for a couple of pennies while families laughed heartily and clapped for them after their energetic dance routines. All these memories became compelling reasons for my siblings and me to want to go back. As children it never occurred to us that circumstances surrounding this second return were quite different, and so would everything else be.

On the eve of our departure from Lagos, the kids were overjoyed, but my parents did not share in our excitement; they somberly walked around, directing our packing activities while we dutifully followed their instructions, throwing our things together in boxes and cartons. It was during the packing exercise that we learnt that my eldest sister, Ijeoma, who was a secondary school student in Lagos then, was going to stay behind and complete the term in school before returning. This sounded absurd to me, but of course I had no say in it. As evening time came, out of tiredness from the all day packing exercise, the kids all fell asleep. I drifted into a restless sleep filled with dreams of what to expect in Nnewi.

In the morning, we must have been woken up before 4:30 a.m. because it was still a little dark. To our surprise, a lorry (*gwongworo*) that was to finally take us home was already loaded with some of our belongings. The lorry was furtively tucked away in one corner to minimize detection by prying eyes that may actually sabotage our plans and deliver us into the hands of *Sajin Major* and his cohorts. We marveled at how the lorry was completely loaded without us waking up, but we never really bothered to ask our parents how the feat was accomplished because there were more important things to be attended to that morning.

The journey to Nnewi was rough; my mother sat in the front with the driver and my younger brother, Nnamdi. The rest of us sat in the back for a journey that seemed to last all day. Sitting in the back of a lorry for such a long journey was not a pleasant experience at all. We were tucked into openings that our belongings did not occupy, and every time the lorry tilted to one side it seemed as though our boxes would dislodge from their shaky positions and fall over us. We took the whole thing in stride, occasionally singing songs we had learnt from my aunt, Mamaocha. We would sing:

Chukwu, anyi ejikere ije nke anyi
Anyi mara na gi bu onye ndu anyi
Oge anyi ga arapu, biko duru anyi
Nani gi kanyi n'atukwasi obi

meaning:

God, we are ready to embark on our journey
We know that you are our guide
When we leave, please guide us
Only you do we put our trust in.

As the sun came up, it was even more miserable. Some parts of the road from Lagos to Onitsha were dusty, but no one cared much, and my mother knew exactly when to ask the driver to stop and hand us refreshments before proceeding. My father did not go with us; the explanation was that he was going to wait a little longer to see if things would get better. If they did not, he would come back to Nnewi with the rest of our belongings and Ijeoma. I wondered in my mind why he was testing his fate; having found out that his safety could no longer be guaranteed in Lagos, one would think that he would be the first to head home. Of course, that was not my father; he believed strictly in Julius Caesar's assertion that "cowards die many times before their deaths." He was not about to be a coward, and at nearly six feet and about 205 pounds, I saw him as a giant of a man; I felt that he could deflect danger just by being around us.

The journey was saddled with several stops at checkpoints, which were manned by stern-looking soldiers. They would briefly climb up to where we were sitting in the back of the lorry, glance around as if they were looking for something specifically, and then get down and ask the driver to go on. We made it safely to Nnewi; I imagine that we got there sometime after 7:00 p.m. It was getting dark and the sound of silence was beginning to descend on Nnewi. As expected, my grandmother and aunts welcomed us very well along with a handful of relatives and neighbors who were looking us over and sometimes hugging us. I was not sure whether they were told about our arrival in advance, but the turnout suggested to me that they knew a thing or two about it. My grandmother kept asking about my father; she was not satisfied with the answer she was getting about his staying a while longer in Lagos; she wondered aloud why he decided to stay back in Lagos in spite of all the things happening in the West and the North. Obviously, my mother had no answers to that, so after a while the issue temporarily went away. At the time, I thought that our stay in Nnewi was going to last for just a couple of months and that things would get back to normal and we would return to Lagos. Little did I know that a 30-month stay that would drastically change my life and the lives of many, and arguably alter the course of our collective destiny, had just begun.

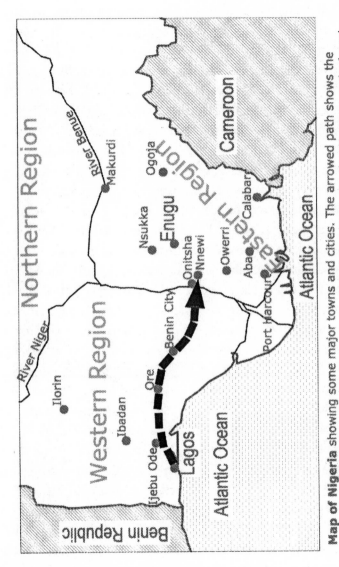

Map of Nigeria showing some major towns and cities. The arrowed path shows the route my family followed, in 1966, when we fled from Lagos(in the Western region) and returned to our hometown Nnewi(in the Eastern region)

Uchenna, Edith and I were quickly enrolled at St. Mary's School, Uruagu Nnewi. St. Mary's school is situated on a vast expanse of land just adjacent to the church building, also called St. Mary's. It was built in an L-shaped configuration with the main field in the front of the building. About 600 feet behind the building was a burial ground which most locals referred to as "bending ground." The road that led from the school building through the cemetery to a small market place called *Olie Ayaka*, always seemed deserted. One of the fables that was bandied about was that at 12:00 noon every day, ghosts in the cemetery would climb out of their resting places and sit on their tombs, soaking in the midday sun! Of course, I had no reason to dispute this story; I felt lucky that I never had to go home through that road. Such were some of the stories we heard then; we took them very seriously and diligently kept away from the cemetery.

At this time, some of the changes that would later become all too familiar in our lives began to occur: I was no longer taken to school in my father's car; instead, we had to walk all the way to and from school. The distance was not far, but the change gave me a glimpse into what was in store for the future and I did not like it one bit! Also, when we were still in Lagos, drinking water (iced water as we called it) was always available in the refrigerator and hot bath water was always available just by turning on the faucet in the bathtub. Here, we had to fetch drinking and cooking water from a spring (called *Okpuani*), which was located about one and a half miles from our house. Sometimes, we even had to take our bath in the spring! To get to the spring, we had to walk through a narrow road that led from the side of our house to a certain point, then descend a very steep hill which eventually led to the spring. My aunt, Irene, began taking me along to the spring to get water; it was always an exhausting experience climbing the hill on our way back. During the first trips, she did not allow me to carry any container, but on the way, I would see kids my age with water containers perfectly balanced on their heads. I became self-conscious that the kids were going to start teasing me for going to the stream empty-handed, so I asked to be given a container. The same was the situation with Uchenna and Edith except Nnamdi who was still too small to do any of that. On the first trip I made with a container, I did okay except for some anxious moments as we climbed back up the hill after fetching water.

Balancing the can on my head took some mastering, but just as with other things, I began to get the hang of it.

The narrow, sandy road that led to the spring was lined on both sides with people's compounds up to a certain point, and then the compounds gave way to bushes called *obachili*. Just before one got to the beginning of the descent to the spring, there was a small, isolated mud house on the left side. The house initially looked deserted to us because we never saw any signs of activity in or around it. One day I asked my aunt if anyone lived in the house; she said yes and described the occupant as a loner, or *okpa nna-kee*, and left it at that. Later on, as we started occasionally going to the stream in the company of other kids, we were told that the inhabitant was called Udemezue. He was described as weird, and even though the kids did not specifically say why he was weird, they gave the impression that you would not want to meet him on the way to the stream alone! I continued to ask what would happen and nobody seemed to know. I filed that story in the back of my mind and felt that no circumstance would make me go to the spring alone.

One day, while I was sleeping, Aunt Irene went to the stream to prepare bitterleaf for making soup. When I woke up, I asked about her and was told that she went to the stream, so I picked up my water can and ran out to join her. Just as I entered the area where houses gave way to bushes, a sudden feeling of fear overtook me; at that very moment, I remembered that the next house was Udemezue's. I was immobilized by fear; going back did not seem feasible and going on was not either. I slowly started walking towards the direction of the stream, praying that all the people that used that road would appear somehow, but I was out of luck—the road was deserted! The time must have been around 6:00 or 6:30 p.m., because dusk was slowly gathering and the sun had receded beyond view. It began to dawn on me that it was a mistake to have left the house at that time of the day to go to the stream. Most people in Nnewi, at that time of the day, would have finished fetching water and would now be at home, pounding cassava and preparing bitter leaf soup for supper. It was not uncommon to hear the sound of mortar pounding cassava while inhaling the whiff of bitter leaf soup, which seemed to be a staple in Nnewi. All this probably explains why the road to the stream seemed deserted. Just as I lurched forward to continue my journey, I heard what sounded like the crackling of tree branches rubbing against one another. I slowly turned to the direction of the sound and sure enough, a middle-aged man with a wry smile on his face was making his way out of the bush toward the narrow road I was on. All he had on was a piece of cloth folded around his waist, double folded around his private area to provide a scanty cover. His dressing was not unusual in Nnewi then. Called *iwa ogodo*, a lot of elderly men dressed that way. He may have had a walking stick in his hand, but I never bothered to find out because at that moment I dropped my water can and ran the fastest race of my life, heading towards the spring. I only ended that race when I met my aunt just as I reached the beginning of the descent towards the spring. In my hurry to get away from someone I felt was Udemezue, I forgot that I ran past a few people who were slowly making their ways from the stream with their water cans balanced on their heads. I was panting and sweating profusely. Befuddled and alarmed by this strange scenario, Aunt Irene inquired what was wrong. I could not immediately tell her what had happened because I was still trying to catch my breath. She then handed me the bitter leaf basket she was clutching in one hand and put her hand on my head as we slowly started walking back the direction from whence I came. After a little while, she asked me again and I replied that I saw Udemezue when I was coming to join her. She was overcome with laughter so violent that she almost dropped the water can she had on her head. At first I was not sure why she found it amusing and then she asked, "How did you know it was Udemezue?" I described the man I saw. She then said that Udemezue was harmless, but that sometimes kids derided him, much to his chagrin. She began to reassure me; the more she talked, the more foolish I felt about my actions. She later admitted that she thought that something had happened at home and I had been asked to come and fetch her.

Before long, we were back in the location where my ordeal started and, as she expected, my water can was still on the side of the path where it fell. I picked it up and we went home. I did not feel comfortable telling Uchenna and Edith what had happened; that would have attracted a lot of teasing. Aunt Irene never talked about it either. She was very protective of me, and that fondness continued for a very long time. As for Udemezue, I do not know what became of the man and I still have no idea who his extended family members were.

We witnessed a lot of ingenuity in Nnewi; in the night, our gaslight was supplemented with light from locally made lighting filaments called *uli*. The filaments were made from the entrails of palm trees; the entrails were doused in and allowed to soak up oil for a while and then dried in the sun for a couple of hours. One *uli* lasted for as much as 30 minutes and provided very good lighting, although it created an unpleasantly strong odor of burning oil in the room. Just as a candle is balanced on a candlestick, the locals designed what they called *njioku*, or light holder, which acted like a candleholder. *Njioku* was a type of tripod constructed from cassava plant stem with three branches on one end and just one stem on the other. A small hole was made on the single stem side of *njioku* and that was where the lighting filament was tucked in and lit up. There was yet another ingenuity to keep drinking water cool; the water was put in earthen pots lined up just behind my grandma's kitchen and the house provided a round-the-clock shadow over the pots. As a result, water from the pots was always cool, although it had a characteristic taste of burnt brick.

The earthen pots that cooled our drinking water also provided a sanctuary, albeit inadvertently, for something else. One day, after getting drinking water from one of the pots with my cup, I stood there drinking it when I detected a "cool" feeling over my feet. At first, I did not pay attention to it; I was very thirsty and was determined to finish the water I had in my cup before doing anything. I noticed, however, that the feeling on my feet was dynamic; it was as though something was crawling over them. I looked down and must have jumped up more than two feet into the air because of what I saw. The cup I had in hand went flying in the other direction. It was a snake! A black and white snake. I almost crushed the snake as I landed back down after jumping up. Aunt Irene, who was standing in the kitchen, ran towards me and when she saw what it was, she just said, "Don't worry, it will not harm you." Perplexed and puzzled, and with my heart still pounding at a million beats per minute, I asked what she meant. In my mind, I was hoping for her to get help to kill the snake, and she was telling me that it would not harm me. She then said it was an abomination to kill a python in Nnewi; she said, "*Eke bu nwadiana.*" She said that if one killed a python, the person had to buy a coffin and bury it like a human being. I could not believe what I was hearing. That was the very first time I ever came that close to a serpent in my life. I remembered that in our Sunday school class in Lagos, we had been told how a serpent (Satan) deceived Eve into eating the forbidden fruit. I had thought that a serpent should always be killed, and here was my aunt telling me it could not be killed. She fetched a stick, allowed the python to crawl onto it and gingerly took it to a nearby bush outside our compound and released it. I kept thinking to myself that there were many surprises for me in Nnewi.

More stories of atrocities against the Igbo people in the North continued to filter in; some reported that trainloads of Igbo people were coming back to the East with maimed, dismembered and some dead Igbos. Apparently, they were the victims of the ongoing genocide in northern Nigeria. Concern for what was happening in the nation was heightening. Igbo families, who had relatives living in the North or the western part of Nigeria, were frantically trying to find out the condition of their relatives. Some traveled to places like Enugu, which was a train terminus, to see if they could get word about their relatives or to see any returning Igbos who could give them information about their relatives. Some would come back with very sad stories of what they saw at the train stations; they talked about seeing people with gouged eyes or with their hands cut off. There were also stories about the massacre of Igbos who had gone to the train stations in the North, hoping to be transported back to the East. They were met at the train stations by angry mobs chanting *"ina nyamili?"* and then clubbed or matcheted to death. Some were even cut down in a hail of bullets. Some people talked about Igbo families they used to know in the North but which were wiped out in the pogrom. As more families continued to return to Nnewi, it struck me that most of the Igbo people who lived in nice houses and government-reserved areas in the townships like Lagos, did not actually have decent houses to live in when they came back to Nnewi. Apparently, many Igbo people, working and making their living in townships, did not see the immediate need to build houses in their hometowns; this proved to be a very costly mistake. You would hear of or see a family that was "stinkingly" rich and living in opulent houses in the townships, but came home to confront the thatch and mud houses that were built by their forebearers. Some had small houses with very limited number of rooms that failed to accommodate all their children. Ancillary structures were sometimes converted into sleeping rooms. In our own case, even though my family had built a four-bed room bungalow about two years earlier, we still had some accommodation problems just because of the sheer size of my immediate family. The presence of my grandparents' house in the same compound helped ease the accommodation problem.

Looking back, one wonders why Igbos did not start building houses that would accommodate their families immediately after they got back to their respective towns in eastern Nigeria in 1966. I suspect that at that point in time, many were still hoping that things would normalize in a few months and that they would all go back to where they used to live. Also, many left their belongings in the townships because they left in a hurry. So, even if they wanted to build houses, they may not have had the wherewithal to do so.

At this time, my brothers, Emmanuel and Fidelis, returned to Nnewi from their respective secondary schools.

I noticed that kids in Nnewi seemed more self-reliant than most of us who had just returned from the townships—*ndi ofia*, as returnees were called. During recess in school, you would see kids making all types of arts and crafts—baskets and brooms. I enjoyed watching them do it. The only part of the schoolwork I never really cared for was cutting the grass in the schoolyard; each kid was given a portion of the field to cut with a machete called *mma akpa*. It was more slender than a regular machete and lighter. The kids who were brought up in Nnewi had become used to that type of work, so they had no trouble completing their tasks. Some of us, straight from the townships, found the task very daunting. In my case, even after managing to complete the task, my palms would be covered with painful blisters. I was internally hoping that the problem in the nation would end as soon as possible so we could go back to Lagos. It bothered me that kids in Nnewi did not seem to care about what was happening in the nation; they went about their businesses as though nothing was really happening. That was a far cry from what happened when we were in Lagos; we always listened to adults talk about the disturbances and then discussed it amongst ourselves. I also found some of the things the kids in Nnewi did very bizarre! There was a boy called *Emeka ugulu*. *Ugulu* was the Igbo name for harmattan. He was called *ugulu* because every time you saw him, his skin, especially his legs, looked very dry and scaly, like those of someone who was in the middle of a severe harmattan season. He walked around the school during recess with several broomsticks and when he came to you, he would hand you a single fresh broomstick and ask that you flog his legs with it. Some people would oblige him and do so while others would hail him. That seemed to be his way of showing that he was strong, but to me, I saw that as the highest form of backwardness and vowed never to partake in that type of "primitive" game.

I began to get the hang of things and started making friends. More children seemed to be joining the school, practically on a weekly basis. Apparently, more Igbo people were returning to the East from the northern and western states to escape the killings and parents wasted no time in enrolling their kids in school right away.

Meanwhile, my father's obduracy in not leaving Lagos with us, proved very costly for the whole family. He was supposed to return with the rest of the properties we left in Lagos, including the new toys he had recently bought for us from a Japanese Math lecturer at the College of Technology. What happened was that after we left Lagos, harassment of Igbo people intensified to an alarming proportion and my father suspected that our house was under surveillance. Coupled with the stories they were hearing about the intensification of abductions and killings, he had to leave Lagos in a hurry without many of our belongings, except a few things he could pack in his car. When he returned, we were happy to see him, but very disappointed when he narrated the story of his ordeal. He ended the story by saying that we would probably not be able to get our things back. We were also disappointed that Ijeoma had not come back with him, for reasons I never could fathom. Again, the explanation was that she needed to finish the term in her school. She was left with my cousin, Joel Aralu, who was still in Lagos at the time. As things continued to worsen, Joel left Lagos and sent my sister to one of my maternal aunts, called Nkili, to live with. Eventually, when the federal soldiers started restricting travel from the federal enclave to the eastern region, it became difficult for my sister to return, and so the struggle to bring her back to Nnewi started. My parents were frantically sending messages to Lagos any way they could to find a way to bring her back. Stories about Igbo people who started the journey back to the East from the federal enclave, but never made it, became rife. All manners of stories were told. Those who returned alive narrated stories of how returnees had to go through several checkpoints manned by stern-faced soldiers. Depending on their mood, they would let people go by, but in some instances, they would take away the man of the house or drag young girls away. Some people had their belongings taken away from them and then allowed to pass through. These horror stories again made my father feel guilty for having made the decision in the first place to leave Ijeoma behind.

In Lagos, Ijeoma was pondering what to do. She had heard what was happening to some of the easterners who tried to go back to the East, so she continued to weigh what her actions should be. It would have been easier for her to stay in Lagos if she had spoken Yoruba language fluently, but she did not and knew that if she stayed behind, sooner than later, she was going to be faced with constant harassment and abuse. One day, she made the decision to brave things and embark on the precarious journey back to Nnewi.

Ijeoma's absence began to cause a lot of concern in our household. It was becoming difficult for us to get reliable news about the state of affairs in Lagos. She was just a teenager and we knew that she was smart and would probably make the right decisions, but the horror stories we were hearing were too gruesome to ignore. We started keeping vigil and conducting prayers in our house, morning and night, for Ijeoma's safe return. After prayers in the night, even after our gas light had been extinguished, we would sit around, listening and hoping that she would come knocking on the front gate.

One evening, after dark, we had just finished our traditional prayers when a loud bang was heard on the outside gate, called *uzo ozodo*. Fidelis ran out to see who it was. At the time in the village, after dark, it was usually rare for people to pay social visits to others. Therefore the loud bang on the door, to us, meant an emergency! We all waited for Fidelis to come back and all of a sudden, a loud shout of *"okwanu Ijeoma"* filled the air. We all rushed out and embraced her. Once in the house, my father asked her what happened, but instead of answering, she said, "please, let us pray first." After the prayer, she told us stories of what happened. She said that when it was finally decided that she was going to take the risk and start coming back to the East, they faced the problem of finding transportation that would expose her to the least amount of danger. At last, they heard that vehicles that still carried mail to the East helped to secretly convey people. Arrangement was made for her to ride in one of the vehicles with the hope that the federal soldiers, who now seemed to be permanently stationed along Lagos-Onitsha road, would not find her. At first, it was assumed that she was going to be the only passenger, apart from the driver, in the mail vehicle, but it turned out that the driver had picked up other people. As a result, they were literally packed like sardines. The journey was uneventful for a while after they left Lagos, but soon they were stopped at every checkpoint. At each checkpoint, the soldiers would look through the vehicle, have strong words with the driver and in the final analysis, remove some people, especially men. At some checkpoints, they were asked to disembark and taken into police posts in town. At these posts, they were interrogated, and people who seemed uncooperative were beaten and removed. In some areas, they passed the night. The nightmare continued and as the journey progressed, less and less of them were left in the vehicle. By the time the vehicle got to Onitsha, three days later, only half of the passengers who started the journey, were still left. The others were beaten and removed by the soldiers. To this day, she feels that those people may have been killed.

My family was overjoyed that Ijeoma returned safely and I am almost certain that my father felt relieved that his mistake had not brought about a deadly consequence.

Lagos, 1964—my family. Front row, from left: Edith, Emmanuel, Uchenna, me, my father, Nnamdi, my mother. Standing fourth from left, Ijeoma, and fifth from left, Fidelis.

1962– Front row: me. Second row, from left: Edith, Uchenna and Ijeoma. Back row, from left: Emmanuel, Caro (our relative) and Fidelis.

1964—My father at the grounds of Yaba College of Technology

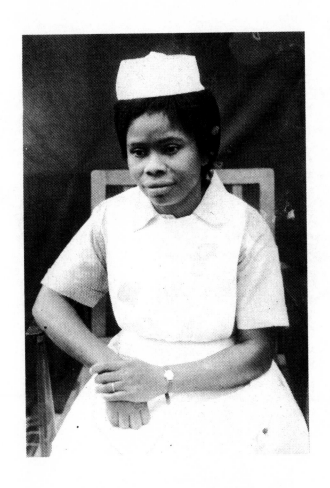

1964—My mother as a young nurse in Lagos

Picture taken in 1990—the family house we lived in during the war. Built in 1964.

My grandmother in Nnewi. Not sure when picture was taken.

3

Biafra Is Declared

Things continued to move at a feverish pace and there was always one sad story or the other about the genocide going on in northern Nigeria. Many Igbos had now returned to Nnewi. At the St Mary's school, my teacher was a dark, very dedicated lady who walked with a noticeable limp and the kids called her *okpa tim,* or "strained leg." In my class, there was a boy called Festus Mbanugo. He was very rascally and unruly and it seemed like he was always ready to fight with anyone in the class. He was full of life and energy and played a lot of pranks. Sometimes, in class, he would crawl under the teacher's desk, and while the teacher talked to the class, oblivious of his presence, he would make funny faces at the class. As a result of his bellicose nature, no one in class would dare to alert the teacher of his mischief. Because of all the energy he exuded, it was a shock when we came to school one day and our teacher announced that Festus had died the night before. She did not say what he died of, but what really sobered us all up was the way that the teacher announced his death. She simply said that he was dead and would not come out again.

I used to sit very close to this boy in class; he was one of those who talked about the burial ground behind our school and how ghosts came out at midday to soak up the sun. I wondered if he had joined the ghosts there. It was not a very pleasant experience for me. Just a couple of weeks after the death of Festus, another tragedy occurred. It was during recess and the class was a beehive of activities. As usual, some pupils were making crafts while others just ran around, playing the hide-and-seek game. The chalkboard, on which our teacher had written our assignment for the next day, was still on the easel. Some boys were playing touch game and in an attempt by one of them to run away from his playmate, named Sunday Azubogu, he inadvertently dislodged the chalkboard from the easel. The edge of the chalkboard landed squarely on Sunday's forehead. Immediately, blood started gushing out of his head and most of the kids took to their heels! I froze momentarily in my tracks; I could not believe the amount of blood that was coming out of his head. In fact, I was almost certain that he would pass out right there, so I was internally hoping that God would spare us the gruesome experience of watching one of our own die a sudden and painful death. I think that one of the children ran out and called our teacher, who was chatting with the other teachers, and they all rushed to the class where Sunday was now keeled over and gasping for breath. They brought a white basin, which was originally placed outside the classroom to catch rainwater for hand washing and laid it directly below Sunday's head to catch his blood. After a while, the blood flow ebbed to a trickle; by then, Sunday had his hands on his waist and was keeled over as though he was about to regurgitate something. He was not crying, but was making a frightening grunting sound.

One of the teachers, who frantically ran towards the direction of the church when he saw what had happened to Sunday, later came back in a vehicle with another man and Sunday was taken away. We were expecting the worst; no one who witnessed the loss of blood and the way he was reacting gave him any chance of survival. For the rest of the day, the kids huddled around, discussing the issue, while the blood splatters on the floor were being cleaned up. We wondered what they would do with the blood in the basin, since they had taken it along with them. One of the kids said that they would put it back in his head but he could not explain to the rest of us how that could be possible. The boy who dislodged that chalkboard had already been taken to the headmaster's office, and we knew what that meant. We were all sorry for him because we knew that he had not done it on purpose.

After a period of absence, Sunday came back to school, to the surprise of the rest of the class. He had a long stitch mark on his forehead and his head seemed to have shrunk in size. The last time I saw him, in the early eighties, he still had that mark, and his head never developed into a regular shape. All these tragedies, coupled with the state of affairs in the nation, were really very frightening. Life continued but increasingly, easterners were agitating for the secession of the eastern region from the rest of Nigeria.

One day, in May of 1967, at the St. Mary's School, news started circulating that the eastern region had finally seceded. It was said that the name of the new nation was Biafra. Suddenly, there was a gathering of many people in the schoolyard; some were carrying cut down branches of trees and others had palm fronds. Spontaneously, a demonstration in support of the secession started. There was commotion! The chanting of war songs filled the air; some people had pictures of Col. Chukwuemeka Odumegwu Ojukwu while singing the song: "Republic Biafra, republic Biafra, republic Biafra, and welcome Biafra." There were people in the crowd who pronounced the name of the new nation as BAYAFRA. They sang other songs like:

Ojukwu nye anyi egbe
Kanyi gbagbue Gowon chelu ndi Awusa
Ojukwu nye anyi egbe
Iwe, iwe dianyi n'obi

meaning:

Ojukwu give us guns
To do away with Gowon and await Hausa
Ojukwu give us guns
There is anger, anger in our hearts.

They also sang:

We shall not, we shall never move,
Just like a tree that's planted by the water
We shall not be moved.
Ojukwu is behind us, we shall never move,
God is behind us, we shall never move…

The crowd was growing by the minute, and suddenly they made a spontaneous decision to go to Col. Odumegwu Ojukwu's residence to show solidarity. Ojukwu's village, called Umudim, is a couple of miles from my own village of Uruagu. I knew that my parents would be mad at me if I followed the demonstrators, so, as soon as they left, I quickly picked up my belongings, joined the rest of the kids, who were as overwhelmed by the turn of events as me, and headed home. School dismissed unceremoniously on that day.

It was much later that I realized what actually triggered the demonstration on that day. In May of 1967, when the easterners could no longer take the killing of their brethren in northern Nigeria, the eastern region house of assembly gave a mandate to Col. Chukwuemeka Ojukwu to declare an independent nation of Biafra. On May 30, he formally declared to the world that the eastern region had become a sovereign nation called Biafra. It was this development that triggered the solidarity demonstration at the St. Mary's school. In his declaration speech, Col. Ojukwu had stated that after all the atrocities the Igbos had endured at the hands of the northerners, there was no basis for continued coexistence of the Igbos and other regions in the country called Nigeria. This news brought joy to the easterners and triggered the spontaneous solidarity demonstrations that ensued.

Below is the full text of the declaration speech on that day by Col. Chukwuemeka Odumegwu Ojukwu (*courtesy, Biafraland.com*):

Fellow countrymen and women, you, the people of Eastern Nigeria: conscious of the supreme authority of Almighty God over all mankind, of your duty to yourselves and posterity;

Aware that you can no longer be protected in your lives and in your property by any government based outside Eastern Nigeria;

Believing that you are born free and have certain inalienable rights which can best be preserved by yourselves;

Unwilling to be unfree partners in any association of a political or economic nature;

Rejecting the authority of any person or persons other than the Military Government of Eastern Nigeria to make any imposition of whatever kind or nature upon you;

Determined to dissolve all political and other ties between you and the former Federal Republic of Nigeria;

Prepared to enter into such association, treaty or alliance with any sovereign state within the former Federal Republic of Nigeria and elsewhere on such terms and conditions as best to subserve your common good;

Affirming your trust and confidence in me;

Having mandated me to proclaim on your behalf, and in your name, that Eastern Nigeria be a, sovereign independent Republic,

NOW THEREFORE I, LIEUTENANT-COLONEL CHUKWUEMEKA ODUMEGWU OJUKWU, MILITARY GOVERNOR OF EASTERN NIGERIA,

BY VIRTUE OF THE AUTHORITY, AND PURSUANT TO THE PRINCIPLES, RECITED ABOVE,

DO HEREBY SOLEMNLY PROCLAIM THAT THE TERRITORY AND REGION KNOWN AS AND CALLED EASTERN NIGERIA TOGETHER WITH HER CONTINENTAL SHELF AND TERRITORIAL WATERS SHALL HENCEFORTH BE AN INDEPENDENT SOVEREIGN STATE OF THE NAME AND TITLE OF,

"THE REPUBLIC OF BIAFRA."

AND I DO DECLARE THAT—

(1) all political ties between us and the Federal Republic of Nigeria are hereby totally dissolved;

(ii) all subsisting contractual obligations entered into by the Government of the Federal Republic of Nigeria or by any person, authority, organization or government acting on its behalf, with any person, authority or organization operating or relating to any matter or thing, within the Republic of Biafra, shall henceforth be deemed to be entered into with the Military Governor of the Republic of Biafra for and on behalf of the government and people of the Republic of Biafra, and the covenants thereof shall, subject to this declaration, be performed by the parties according to their tenor;

(iii) all subsisting international treaties and obligations made on behalf of Eastern Nigeria by the Government of the Federal Republic of Nigeria, shall be honored and respected;

(iv) Eastern Nigeria's due share of all subsisting international debts and obligations entered into by the Government of the Republic of Nigeria on behalf of the Federation of Nigeria shall be honored and respected;

(v) steps will be taken to open discussions on the question of Eastern Nigeria's due share of the assets of the Federation of Nigeria and personal, properties of the citizens of Biafra throughout the Federation of Nigeria;

(vi) the rights, privileges, pensions, etc., of all personnel of the Public Services, the Armed Forces and the Police now serving in any capacity within the Republic of Biafra, are hereby guaranteed;

(vii) we shall keep the door open for association with, and would welcome, any sovereign unit or units in the former Federation of Nigeria Or in any other parts of Africa desirous of association with us for the purposes of running a common services organization and for the establishment of economic ties;

(viii) we shall protect the lives and property of all foreigners residing in Biafra; we shall extend the hand of friendship to those nations who respect our sovereignty, and shall repel any interference in our internal affairs;
(ix) we shall faithfully adhere to the charter of the Organization of African Unity and of the United Nations Organization;

(x) it is our intention to remain a member of the British Commonwealth of Nations in our right as a sovereign, independent nation.

LONG LIVE THE REPUBLIC OF BIAFRA!
AND MAY GOD PROTECT ALL WHO LIVE IN HER.

Of course the Nigerian government did not accept the secession bid, and so they mobilized soldiers against the new nation of Biafra. In July 1967, the Biafra war began in earnest. I still remember the events of that day in 1967 as though they just occurred yesterday! I must confess, though, that the thought that many of the young men who participated in that demonstration perished in the war still sends a cold chill down my spine! They were full of energy; they started with hope, with enthusiasm and with the feeling that since the Igbos had been wronged by the northerners, debased, trampled upon and were on the brink of total annihilation—the eastern region had no other choice than to defend herself. Some were university undergraduates who had returned to Nnewi as a result of the pogroms; others were graduates who were already gainfully employed in different walks of life; some were businessmen, fathers, uncles and cousins. They perished in a war that could probably have been averted. I still get teary-eyed when I remember those young men; my heart continues to go out to the families who lost these brave men; men who gave their lives so that others could live. God bless their families and give their souls eternal repose.

After the declaration of Biafra, civil defense and combing activities started picking up steam in Nnewi. In my clan of Okpunoeze, the town crier, whose responsibility it was to disseminate information to all about activities related to the war, was very busy. He normally started to make his round just after dark, when the sound of cassava-pounding mortars had abated. He would sound his small metal gong, called *ogene*, three times, and then say something like: *anakpo oku n'Iba, na six o'clock nke ututu echi, onye abiaghi ya, oranra ego ise*. Meaning: a meeting has been summoned in the village square (*Iba*) at six o'clock tomorrow morning; absentees will pay a penalty of five shillings. At the time, I always wondered why the town crier was not afraid to be wandering around in the dark alone. What if he runs into ghosts? I thought. I also wondered why he said everything else in Igbo but then said six o'clock in English. Don't we have a way in Igbo of saying six o'clock? I wondered.

Any day that the elders would meet, my father would wake up very early, conduct our morning devotion and set out for the short walk to *Iba*. My uncle, Godwin, also went along with him.

It took a while before the kids started finding out what the frequent meetings at *Iba* were about. Iba was the primary gathering location for elders even before the eastern region seceded. After the Declaration of Biafra, it was being used as a place for strategizing on what part my village people would play in the event of a war. The meeting building was rectangular in shape, with the shorter side facing the entrance to the square. The interior walls were decked out with Nnewi artifacts, like masks and beads, and generally conveyed an eerie feeling to me, probably because of the absence of ample natural lighting in it. Talking drums and large wooden gongs occupied one corner of the meeting room and I always wondered what those were for. Meeting attendees usually sat in a U-shaped formation, facing the facilitator, who was also the head of *Iba*. The men who attended the meetings, on return, always talked about the progress of what was happening in Biafra. They were also gearing up for war. Some carved mock guns out of sticks and carried them around.

A rumor that seemed to permeate every facet of Nnewi at that time was that traitors could be lurking in our midst. Part of what was being discussed in *Iba*, therefore, was how to fish out the traitors and flush them out of Biafra. Consequently, an activity that was referred to as "combing" was instituted. One day, very early in the morning, men from our villages gathered in the square. They were armed with machetes, mock guns, double barrel guns and the like. One could tell by the way they heartily chattered and carried on that they loved the mission they were about to embark on. After getting initial briefings from their leaders, they organized themselves into groups, and while chanting war songs, headed into adjacent bushes—the combing exercise had begun. We were told that they were looking for the enemy, or for traitors. They came back late in the day, exhausted, but satisfied that they had answered the clarion call to defend their homeland. It was patriotism at its height. I cannot say whether those combing activities yielded any tangible results, but I know that it made some of us feel a little safer; our men were taking necessary steps to keep us out of harm's way, we felt.

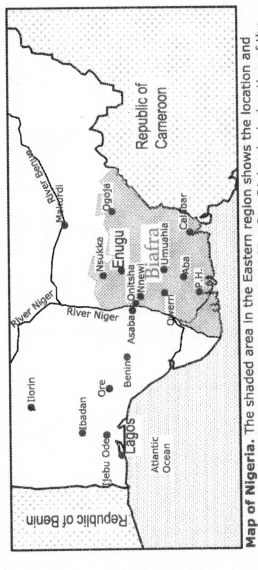

Map of Nigeria. The shaded area in the Eastern region shows the location and general size of the nation of Biafra in May 1967, after Ojukwu's declaration of the sovereign nation of Biafra.

4

Fidelis Goes to War

Fierce fighting was now going on in several places inside Biafra like Obolo Eke, Obolo Afor, Opi Junction, Eha Amufu and others around the Nsukka area, but because of the fact that the war theaters were far removed from Nnewi, we were not experiencing the agony and deprivation that others close to the warfronts were. These towns are located on the northern fringes, closest to the border between Biafra and Nigeria. They were therefore the first targets attacked by the federal troops. Those who witnessed fighting in the towns, or who lived close to them, told frightening stories of how deafening sounds of artillery barrages and small arms fire always filled the air. They complained that mortar shells sometimes exploded in their villages, killing innocent civilians and damaging buildings; it was the reason why they had to pack up their belongings and leave, thereby becoming refugees in Biafra. That marked the first time I personally heard the word "refugee." Some people inadvertently pronounced it as *lofuji*, which gave it another connotation in Igbo language meaning, "people who forgot their yam." The stories from the refugees always sounded very demoralizing but we took solace in the fact that Biafran soldiers were said to be holding their own and matching the federal troops fire for fire.

During this period, Fidelis was in the habit of periodically visiting Onitsha; he liked to get first-hand information about the progress of the war and how the Biafrans were doing. On return, he would tell us what he had learned and assess the progress. On one of those days, he came back and reported that Dennis Memorial Grammar School Onitsha had been hit. I do not recall if he said it was mortar or bomb, but he sounded infuriated by the turn of events. He loved Onitsha very much. Prior to the beginning of the war, he used to spend some of his holidays with aunt Mamaocha in Onitsha, where she worked as a caterer at the Dolphin Café Hotel. Dennis Memorial Grammar School or DMGS was one of the premier and most prestigious secondary schools in the then eastern region and had produced many renowned Igbos. With the school now in the line of fire, many Igbos felt somewhat violated because it signified an assault on their collective dignity.

The war continued and later, as a result of his passion for the Biafran cause, Fidelis announced his intention to join the army. We were all apprehensive about this; he was only 17 years of age and my family felt that he was too young to go to war, an opinion he rejected outright! He saw the killing of easterners in northern Nigeria as an abominable crime that had to be avenged. He always spoke movingly about the case of the pregnant Igbo woman who was disemboweled in the North at the height of hostilities; the woman's unborn child was said to have been removed and killed along with her. This story made its round in most parts of Biafra and played a big part in the decision of some young men who joined the Biafran army. Like them, Fidelis did not see any compromise with people who were barbaric and sadistic enough to inflict such suffering on humankind. Every time my father tried to dissuade him from joining the army, in his usual ebullient manner, Fidelis would tell him that he would oblige on the condition that my father, who was in his late forties at the time, would go to war in his place.

Born in the northern Nigerian city of Jos, Fidelis started right from his childhood days to exhibit an uncanny sense of courage. He ventured into areas where most kids would not and did things that most kids would be afraid to even contemplate. He was the protector of his younger siblings, Ijeoma and Emmanuel. When they were growing up in Jos he would always stand guard at public taps where they fetched drinking water to ensure that no one abused or deprived his siblings the opportunity to get water when it was their turn. He sometimes did things that seemed like he was testing the limits of his strength; he once threw up an iron ball into the air and used his head to catch it while other kids watched in horror! Of course he sustained very serious injury on the head that required several stitches to close. He received the stitches without anesthesia to serve as a deterrent from doing similar things in the future.

At the Merchants of Light Secondary School, he was a dedicated Boy Scout and enjoyed the many jamborees they embarked on. He was also in the boxing club where, once again, he displayed a sense of courage that won him the admiration of all. All in all, in spite of his intimidating personality, he was a gentle soul who hated injustice. He particularly hated to see women persecuted and also detested bullies who preyed on weaker people. He easily went to bat for the weaker person and would fight if need be. His peers used to characterize him as someone who had "single bone," a reference to his sheer strength.

It was therefore not surprising to my family when Fidelis opted to go to war in spite of his young age. He felt that Nigeria was the bully in this instance, and he was as confident as ever that Nigeria's encounter with Biafra was going to be similar to that of the biblical David and Goliath. My mother's protests failed to change his mind about joining the army.

Fidelis finally won the argument and joined the Biafra militia for initial training. At this time, enlistment of new recruits was going on all over Biafra and young men were joining in droves. Morale was very high because we were hearing very encouraging stories about the gallantry of Biafran soldiers in the warfront. At one time, we heard that the Biafran army had crossed the Niger Bridge into the midwestern region and were marching towards the capital city of Nigeria, Lagos. Biafran scientists were also said to have hunkered down and were working round the clock to develop weapons that would help Biafra win. Meanwhile, at the recruitment depots, younger men who went to join the army were being turned back on account of their youth. Some continued to go to the training depot on a frequent basis just to see if the recruiters would change their minds. Most days, Fidelis would come back from militia training and start practicing some of the parade techniques they were taught, including how to handle guns and dive for cover. He had a wooden gun with which he practiced and we were all very proud of him.

One day, he came back from the militia training and had a very worried look on his face. We were all concerned and wondered what had drastically altered his usual ebullient and optimistic countenance. When asked what the problem was, at first he did not say much. When he saw that we were not going to relent, he opened up. He said that at the militia training that day, intelligence report revealed that Nigeria was about to "shoot" a deadly chemical into the air. That chemical, he said, would gradually kill people who inhaled it. He said that Biafran scientists quickly came up with a neutralizer, which was to be prepared by gathering palm fronds, specific types of dried wood and other ingredients I can no longer remember. The mixture was to be burned and the ashes ground together into powder. In the event of a chemical attack, we were to put some of the powder into porous materials like handkerchiefs and start breathing through them to neutralize the effect of the chemical.

As I listened to this story, I could not help but be impressed by the quickness of Biafran scientists in immediately discovering a supposed "antidote." In my mind, it reinforced the story we had been hearing that Biafra had the biggest and best concentration of great minds in Africa. We had distinguished scientists, doctors, lawyers, engineers and brilliant soldiers. I was proud of Biafra and one could sense the feeling of pride in Fidelis as he talked about Biafran scientists and the antidote; his eyes would come aglow and he would gesticulate expansively with his hands. He sincerely believed that with such talents, Biafra would prevail. He never shirked any task he perceived as his responsibility because he felt that while the scientists and soldiers were playing their respective roles, he also had his own part to play. He did not believe in procrastination, so he ended his story by saying that he would start preparing the neutralizer the next day.

Very early the next morning, he was out in our farmland, or *mbubo*, gathering the requisite materials. Even though there was a perimeter wall separating our compound from the farmland, we could hear him whistling some of his favorite war tunes, which he had learnt in the militia. Anytime he resorted to whistling, I could tell that he was either happy about something or was doing something he really loved. He came in later with a bundle of materials all tied together with a type of string we called *ekwele*. Later in the day, he placed them all on a piece of corrugated metal, in the open, behind my grandmother's kitchen and started a bonfire. The fire burned as we all watched curiously, wondering what all that would come to. During the interim, he entertained us with his military parade techniques. With his mock gun in hand, he would belch out the order, "attention" and then stand at attention. He would follow that with "stand at ease" and react accordingly. Something he always said then that took me a while to understand, sounded like, "*ajuwaya*." Every time he said that, he would sort of relax his body and loosely place his mock gun on his side with one end resting on the ground. I later understood that he was saying, "As you were."

When the bonfire simmered down and cooled off, he gingerly collected all the ashes and charcoal and started grinding them all together on Aunt Irene's grinding stone. As he finished grinding each batch into powder, he scooped them together and placed them in a container. You could see fine mist of the powder rising up in the air; he was breathing it all, but did not seem to care. After a while, he started coughing sporadically, but each time my mother asked if he was okay, he would play down the seriousness of the cough. As time passed, he started complaining of a "stinging" headache. At this point, he was urged to stop and my mother gave him some medication, after which he suspended the operation and went to get some rest. The headache persisted for quite a while and he had to miss his militia practice the next day.

When he came back from militia, on the second day after recuperation, we gathered around him, as usual, but could not believe what he had to say. Another intelligence report came in and it turned out that the supposed neutralizer was actually poison and, if inhaled in large amounts, could kill! He said that Nigeria used saboteurs in Biafra to disseminate the hoax in order to cause massive deaths and break the fighting spirit of the people. This baffled everyone and my family made an immediate decision to dig a hole on the ground and bury the remnants of the poison. Right there and then, it became clear that the Biafran war was going to be fought in many fronts, both physical and psychological.

This incident did not shake Fidelis' resolve to join the army. He diligently continued his militia training and made it a point of duty to rehearse what they were taught whenever he came back home. One day, he came back with one of my maternal uncles, called Ezengozi. My mother is from Asaba in the Midwest and Ezengozi was in the town when the federal troops marched into it. He fled the town and ended up in a refugee camp, where Fidelis saw him and brought him home to live with us in Nnewi. Not too long after that, Fidelis joined the regular army at the same time that some of his buddies, like Alphonso Agbodike and Joseph Agbasi (of the blessed memory), were enlisting. On the day of his departure for full military duties, we were all very emotional about it but he smiled broadly as if to assure everyone that things would be okay. My father brought out one of his most prized possessions and handed it to Fidelis. They were a pair of military booths, which were assigned to him when he led cadet students of Yaba College of Technology, as their welfare officer, to their military orientation exercise in the northern Nigerian city of Jaji. That happened sometime in 1965. During that visit to Jaji, my father was also given a full set of Nigerian military uniforms and even participated in the target shooting training with the students.

Fidelis gladly accepted the boots, thanked my father, waved goodbye to all of us and quickly left the compound. As the war progressed, he later made it into the Biafran Commando, Ahoda Stroke Force and the next time he showed up at home, he was in full military regalia, with a gun he called a "setima" to match. Young Fidelis had seen action in the warfront and had become a second lieutenant!

1965—Fidelis during a Boy Scouts photo session at the Merchants of Light School, Oba

Fidelis, during a Boy Scouts jamboree.

As Fidelis and other young men went off to war, we were full of hope that Biafra would prevail. We were exceedingly enamored by what we heard that the commandos could do, so we always spent time singing commando songs we learned, like:

Biafra kunie, buso Nigeria agha
N'ihi na ha bu, ndi namaro Chukwu
Anyi emelie ndi Awusa
Ndi namaro Chukwu
Tigbue ha, zogbue ha
Welu nwude Yakubu

meaning:

Biafra, get up and fight Nigeria
Because they are people who do not know God
We will defeat Hausa
People who do not know God

Beat them, trample on them
And then catch Yakubu (Gowon)

Another song went thus:

Ojukwu bu eze Biafra
Edelu ya na Aburi [Ghana]
Awolowo, Yakubu Gowon
Enweghi ike, imeli Biafra
Biafra win the war
Armored car, shelling machine, heavy artillery
Ha enweghi ike imeli Biafra

meaning:

Ojukwu is the leader of Biafra
It was written in Aburi [Ghana]
Awolowo, Yakubu Gowon
They would not be able to defeat Biafra

The insignia on the commando uniform, depicting a human skull, earned them the name, *isi okpukpu commando* (skull-headed commandos). They were said to be so tough that they were only drafted to the toughest battlefields; we looked at them in awe and that continued to beef up our confidence that Biafra would prevail.

School had stopped temporarily in Nnewi because, school compounds were being converted into living quarters for Biafran war refugees. Many people were now increasingly being displaced from other towns, like Enugu, Nsukka, Aba, Asaba, Calabar and Port Harcourt. These towns had either fallen into the hands of the federal troops or were being threatened; Nigerian troops were unleashing unbridled air and land assault on Biafra. The closure of schools created a situation where kids played all day for lack of any other constructive things to do. Nnamdi and I would leave our house in the morning, after breakfast, and go to a place we called *Anaoji*. It was another square where kids from my village gathered and played. It was very convenient because there was a very tall and large tree on one end of the square we called *ube okpoko*. The tree provided round-the-clock canopy from the scorching midday sun and also produced an edible type of fruit which we ate as we played. Every one of the kids carefully kept away from the base of the tree because it housed all types of ritualistic paraphernalia, such as carved masks and cola nuts. We were told that the tree was sacred and marked the area from where children who died in my village reincarnated. Story had it that the tree could not be cut down, otherwise, the village would suffer serious consequences.

Nnamdi and I only went home from *Anaoji*, which was a very short walk from our house, when we got hungry after midday. In most cases, when we returned home, Ijeoma would force us to take our baths before being given anything to eat. Of course we usually snuck out again after lunch, back to *Anaoji*, to pick up where we left off. There were some kids who seemed to stay there all day and left the square in the evening time only to return promptly the next morning. It surprised me that their parents did not seem to care about their whereabouts. One of our playmates, called Emmanuel Anaike, used to feel embarrassed because anytime his mother wanted him home, she would call out his name from her house in a very loud voice. Their compound was about a five-minute walk from *Anaoji* and her voice would echo in the square as she belched out his name—Emmanel-e-e-e. Once she started calling him, the kids in the square would start teasing Emmanuel. To make his mother stop, he would answer, nne-e-e-e and quickly run out of the square to join her. We also teased him about his little sister, Philomena; she was about six years old but did not seem to have any qualms about walking around naked all day. Every time I saw her, I always wondered why her parents seemed not to care. Emmanuel was, however, very versed in stories about Nnewi and never missed an opportunity to tell us what he knew.

There was a small masonry block building with corrugated metal roofing adjacent to *Anaoji*. The interior consisted of plain cement-plastered walls with a chalkboard crookedly hung on one of them. It had no ceiling covering and so the roof-supporting beams and rafters were exposed. We used to go into the building to play and sometimes embark on gymnastics that involved hanging onto one of the beams and swinging back and forth for a while before letting go and somersaulting onto the floor below. It was always fun. The building was called *nta akara* and Nnamdi used to attend kindergarten class there before schools closed.

During this period, a refugee family moved into our neighbor's house. They had kids our age; the boy was called Ejima and the girl Idowu (she had a Yoruba name). We welcomed the kids with open hands and quickly started playing with them. Idowu was a cute girl, about a year younger than I was, and I liked her. I started keeping my distance from her because I discovered that she talked too much. Within a very short time after their arrival in Nnewi, she seemed to know or pretend to know everything about everybody and I did not like that type of disposition. I felt that if she became aware of the fact that I had a crush on her, the whole village would know instantly; I was not ready to deal with the teasing that would follow. Ejima was also outgoing, but very troublesome. He fought at the slightest provocation. Because of this, most of our playmates did not like him and so he was really not accepted into our playing circle. He resorted to intimidation and always waylaid those of us who had to pass by their compound on our way to *Anaoji*. From the bush, he would pelt us with stones and make silly remarks at us. We all ignored him and that seemed to infuriate him even more.

We used to conduct juvenile arbitration between kids that we felt were at loggerheads or did not just get along. Minor things usually brought about rifts; if a kid insulted another kid's family or parents, the one on the receiving end would instantly stop talking to the errant kid. There was a popular song we sang to deride someone we had fallen out of favor with and it went thus:

Onye ilom sina munaya esego
Chukwu ma n'onwero ife mmere ya
Agam emesi ya ike
Ya buru ozu onweya gaba.

meaning:

My enemy said that we should go our separate ways
God knows that I did nothing to him
I will punish and deal with him
Let him carry his carcass and get away from me

The enmity did not usually last very long because, as soon as other kids got wind of it, the two people involved would be invited to *Anaoji* and asked to shake hands, say each other's names and then bring the disagreement to closure. All these activities occupied our time and after a while became routine.

One day, we were all playing in the square when a car slowly pulled up to the center and stopped. Because we were not used to cars driving into the square, everyone's attention was fixed on the car and the occupants. It had four passengers in it, with some personal belongings occupying a portion of it. Slowly, the front door opened and a woman came out; she walked towards where we were and asked for directions to Uzokwe's compound. We directed her and went back to play, but in my mind I was wondering who they might have been. That thought immediately evaporated as I quickly immersed myself in what I was doing before. Later in the evening, when Nnamdi and I went back home to our compound, we noticed that the car we had earlier seen at the square was now parked in front of our compound. As we entered the house, we also saw that the people we had earlier directed to our house were still there. They were all sitting in the verandah and talking with my parents. We casually greeted them and went to the kitchen to get something to eat. I could not help but notice that our visitors included two kids, a boy and a girl. The girl looked a little younger than me but the boy looked like he would be about my age, although he was taller.

At the kitchen, I asked Ijeoma who the visitors were and she said that they were our relatives from Asaba. The older woman was my mother's stepmother and the younger woman was my mother's sister. Of course, the two kids were our cousins. When Ijeoma added that they were going to be living with us for a while, I was ecstatic. She said that Nigerian soldiers had overrun the town where they lived before and so they had come to seek sanctuary in Nnewi. I was happy that Nnamdi and I would now have other kids to play with inside the compound. The younger woman was Mrs. Maria Edozien; the boy was Charles Edozien and the girl Obiageli Edozien. I continued to think to myself that we had more relatives in Asaba than we had ever met. When I finished my meal, I went back to the verandah and formally approached the boy; we became friends immediately. We went off to a corner and I asked him what his full name was. He said it was Charles Ibegbunam Chibuzor. I, in turn, told him that my full name was Alfred Obiora Chkwukadibia. We immediately engaged in a game of rattling off each other's names and seeing who could do it fastest.

The arrival of Charles and Obiageli became a source of immense happiness for Nnamdi and me. We were all in the same age range and could easily do a lot of things together, and we did. We told stories, played hide-and-seek games and even played war games, depicting Biafra as the winner. Charles, Nnamdi, my other cousin, Emeka, and I would hide under tables and play war games. Charles would play the role of General Ojukwu, I would be Col. Achuzia, Nnamdi would play Achuzia *nta* and Emeka would play Col. Chude Sokei. My uncle Ezengozi helped make life even livelier for us. Along with my brother Emmanuel, they set up a game we called *ncholokoto* in our family meeting building called *ozobi*. We spent time somedays playing the game and it helped remove from our minds, even if momentarily, the horror of the war. Ezengozi also spent time tutoring us; we started using our *ozobi* for studies. He placed Charles, Obiageli and I in his elementary three class, Edith in elementary five and Uchenna in elementary six. He methodically ensured that what he was teaching us was at the class level in which he had placed us. This changed our direction a little bit; Nnamdi and I no longer had to go to *Anaoji* everyday.

During the initial stages of the war, despite the increase in cases of displacement of Biafrans from the towns where they lived, hope was still sky-high for us because of the many heroic feats Biafran soldiers were said to be performing in the warfronts. My aunt, Mamaocha, would come back and tell stories of how Biafran soldiers battled the federal troops, killed many and captured many war machines and guns. We heard that most of the arms and munitions Biafran soldiers were using had been captured from the federal troops, and we were ecstatic about that. The most interesting stories included stories of air raids that were carried out by the federal troops. Mamaocha insisted that all the bombs they dropped on Biafrans either did not explode or missed their targets. In our minds, therefore, we felt that the story we heard, which suggested that the northerners were uncivilized and knew very little about technology, was true. We hoped that their ignorance would persist until we cleverly won the war.

Optimism about Biafra's survival later started dissipating slowly when more families began to get news of the killing of their loved ones in action. Many a time you would suddenly hear a loud wail from a nearby family; further inquiry would reveal that their loved one had been killed. The sight of mothers crying and mourning their sons was always heartbreaking for me; it always reminded me of the fact that my teenage brother was in the army. I could not imagine what would become of my own mother if Fidelis were killed

My father was so concerned by the rise in the death toll of Biafran soldiers that he went looking for Fidelis. He later found him in one of the army camps in the war theater; he was recuperating from malaria. My father asked him to accompany him back home so that my mother would attend to him medically. He refused and told my father that other soldiers do get sick and left for the warfront as soon as they felt better and he would do the same. My father was disappointed, but was proud of the fact that he had given Biafra a brave soldier who assiduously tackled any obstacle that stood between him and his goal of defending his beloved nation.

5

Hunger in Biafra

When the Biafran war first started, I doubt that it occurred to many that hunger was going to be a major factor. This was especially true of Nnewi. There was subsistence farming, with families planting yam, cocoayam, cassava, maize and other foodstuffs. In fact, most people produced enough food to feed their families and even sell the excess in Nkwo Nnewi market. As the war progressed and as refugees who had been displaced from various parts of Biafra arrived in Nnewi to seek sanctuary from the atrocious havoc the federal troops were visiting on them, subsistence farming was no longer sufficient to sustain the teeming population of the town.

The refugees, and even some indigenes of Nnewi, started to look for other means of subsistence. Snail, or *ejula,* which used to be found in abundance in the area, freely roaming the bushes when we first returned from Lagos, suddenly became an endangered species. Snail became scarce because it was now being sought after as a major food source by all. Even people who had never tasted it before then developed a liking for it, albeit reluctantly. It dawned on me that things had deteriorated badly when some of the kids started picking up, roasting and eating the small-sized snail we called *mpiolo*. The only use we had for that size of snail (before things got really bad) was for the shell; we used it to carve conical shaped objects called *okoso*. The kids played with *okoso* by positioning the tapered end on the ground and spinning it around. The challenge was to see who could spin it fastest. War exigency and absolute necessity had, however, turned *mpiolo* into an edible delicacy which was now fiercely sought after, chiefly because the big-sized snail had all but disappeared in the face of mounting desire for it.

Scarcity of food in Biafra forced some of her women folk to engage in what was referred to as *afia attack*. It simply means, "trading in the war zone behind enemy lines." The women went behind enemy lines to buy needed foodstuffs and then returned to Biafra and sold them to the starving masses. It was a very dangerous venture; some of the women never returned from the trip—some were caught in crossfire while others were maltreated by federal soldiers, raped and even killed. It was bad enough that some women had lost their husbands in the warfront and were left with no one to fend for the family. But when hunger threatened to end their lives and those of the children they now had to care for as widows, they had no choice but to venture into *afia attack*.

Some of the women were successful in the trade and came back into Biafra with foodstuffs to sell to the starving masses. There was a particular woman who usually brought delicacies like fresh fish and dried fish (*azu mangala*) as well as sponge and other items that my mother would buy for the family. One day, we came back to find the woman comfortably seated on a small stool in my grandmother's kitchen. In front of her was a white basin, and my mother was standing very close to the basin talking to her. As usual, we thought that she had brought fresh fish, but when I approached where they were and looked at the basin which was filled with water, I noticed a very unusual, meandering movement. I could not at first tell what I had seen. I went a little closer and what I saw shocked me to the core; they were small, black, snake-like creatures, meandering through the water in the basin. My mother and the woman noticed the alarm on my face and turned their attention towards me momentarily. In utter confusion, I asked, "What are those snakes for and what are they doing in the basin?" The woman smiled wryly and said to me, "They are not snakes, they are called *ukolo*, and they are edible; many families in Biafra eat them." She then added, "I brought them for your mother to buy so that you people would try it." As if to prove her point about the "snakes" being edible, she pointed to the end of the kitchen to a stack of the snake-like creatures with sticks, or *mkpisi*, threaded through them. Those ones had already been dried as you would dry fish over the fire. I had had enough! I beckoned on Uchenna and Edith and alerted them to what was happening, and when they saw what I had seen, as if planned and in unison, we all declared to my mother, "We would never eat this, no matter the circumstance."

Throughout this drama, my mother never said a word but was just watching our reaction. Once we said this, she turned to the lady and said, "I told you that nobody would eat this in this house." I could see disappointment on the face of the woman as she slowly started gathering her things to leave. As she did that, she was muttering something like "everybody eats *ukolo*." I later found out that she was right about the fact that many families were eating *ukolo* without qualms. At the end of the war, there was a popular song that went "*mmelizi ukolo, so omina,*" which means, "I will no longer eat *ukolo*, only *omina*." (I think omina was another delicacy.) The moral of the song to me was that people ate *ukolo* only because of war exigencies and felt liberated after the war when they no longer had to.

I do not know what Biafra could have done without CARITAS? CARITAS was a relief agency that brought foodstuffs into Biafra to help the starving masses. They supplied cornmeal, milk, stockfish, egg yolk, rice Gabon and the like. In fact, in appreciation of their generosity, there was a song Biafrans sang in their name which went, "*CARITAS, si anyi, taba okporoko, kwashiorkor g'ana,*" meaning: "CARITAS, asked us to eat stockfish, *kwashiorkor* will stop." The relief food items were very limited in quantity and the fact that officials given the responsibility of distributing it to the hungry masses did not do so equitably exacerbated an already bad situation. The officials sometimes kept some of the relief items to themselves and their families while some people went hungry. I always felt bad at the sight of refugees at the St. Mary's School compound, struggling to get food from the distribution center in an adjacent building. I abhorred the fact that people who were already hungry and had lost strength had to fight to get relief food. It became survival of the fittest; those who were strong enough to shove others out of the way got more rations and those who had become exceedingly weak because of hunger could not get enough food.

Hunger notwithstanding, we did everything normal kids did—we went to boy scouts and choir—but as weeks turned into months, a strange phenomenon started manifesting itself in the kids. Some kids started developing bloated bellies, bloated feet and lighter skin color! The transmogrifying effect of this strange phenomenon on people was drastic. At first, some kids (including me) found this amusing because we did not understand the full implications of what was happening. We would often play with the kids afflicted with this ailment and jokingly call them "*afo mmili ukwa,*" another way of saying that someone is a gourmand or big bellied. We never knew that they were gradually being condemned to an untimely death because of a war they did not cause. We got our rude awakening when some of them actually started dying. A kid you played with in school would progressively start changing in color, like someone afflicted with jaundice. The cheeks would start puffing out, followed by the feet; then the hair would begin to thin out and assume a fine texture while turning reddish brown. The end point is that the child slows down from weakness and eventually dies. I particularly remember Augustine (maybe some of my classmates from then, like Nwakaego Nzekwu, Joy Odunukwe, Chukwudi Ngwube, Uzo Ike, Georgina Obiazi, Anaemenam and others would still remember this incident). Our classroom was the ozobi or meeting place of one Michael Mbonu in a place called Umumeagbu. Augustine had gradually developed puffy cheeks and bloated legs, and even though he used to be dark-colored in complexion, his color started changing. Admittedly, he was a naturally quiet boy, but as this ailment progressed, he no longer participated in our childish shenanigans. During break time, he would just sit by himself away from others.

One day at school he was so quiet that I could tell that he was not feeling any better at all although I never asked. On this day, he again failed to participate in any recreational activities, and later on he regurgitated some of what he had eaten. We all stood around as our teacher tried to help him. When we all arrived in class the next day, Augustine was not on his chair. Minutes later, our teacher ambled in somberly, neither saying anything nor commenting on Augustine's absence. In hushed tones however, we got news that Augustine was dead. I am not exactly sure who broke the news, but Augustine's half-brother, who was also in my class, was absent that day. To think that someone we had all played with not too long before was gone forever was heartbreaking. After school that day, I deliberately went by Augustine's house to verify things for myself, even though I could have used a shortcut to get to my house faster. As I got to the front of his house, there were many people going in and out, and I knew then that the news was true. I cursed those who started the war and prayed to God to punish them duly. I was powerless to do anything; all I could do was go home sad that day and cry. Augustine was no more, but this was not a peculiar episode; it was repeating in many places in Nnewi and Biafra; it was the price of war, a war that was fought so unconventionally that innocent civilians, women and children, were denied food.

After Augustine's death, I began to fully appreciate the effort my parents had been making since the war started to ensure that our family did not suffer malnutrition. My mother did everything possible to make sure that we ate nutritionally rich foods that would save us from the dreaded *kwashiorkor*. She said that the disease was caused by protein deficiency, and so made sure that every member of the family had adequate dose of protein-rich food. First, she mandated the intensification of subsistence farming in my family. Emmanuel, Ezengozi and I cultivated essential foodstuffs when the season came. We usually went to our farmland, called *ubi*, to cultivate yam. I was not strong or big enough to make the earthen mounds in which the yam was sown, so Ezengozi and Emmanuel would make the mounds with their hoes while I followed behind, sowing not just the yam tubers but dried maize and cassava stems in the numerous mounds they made. The cassava stems would eventually sprout and produce cassava, which we used to make *garri*. Garri is rich in carbohydrates. Sometimes, I had to sprinkle the seeds of a vegetable we called "green" on the mounds. The vegetable was used to make a variety of delicacies and my mother always insisted that everyone should have substantial helpings of the vegetable because, as she used to put it, "It will help keep *kwashiorkor* away." Making the earthen mounds for the yam was a very grueling task; first the land had to be tilled with the hoes, and then the mound was made by scooping the soil together into a large heap.

Regardless of the energy-sapping nature of the yam mound-making process, Ezengozi liked it because he got direct benefit out of it. There was a cricket-like creature, called *abuzu*, which was found in abundance as the land was tilled; they lived in holes in the ground, and as the holes were disturbed, they would crawl out and Ezengozi would catch them with minimal effort and place them in a container. By the end of the day, he would have caught as many as twenty of them or more. He would then make a small fire, roast them right there and eat them. He said that *abuzu* was a veritable source of protein. I did not like abuzu and so never partook in it.

As the yams began to sprout, we would tend them with supporting sticks, or *alulu*, on which the stems climbed. We would continue to tend the yam, cassava and vegetable until harvest time, when we removed them, saved some for the next planting season and ate the rest.

My parents also emphasized the need to ensure that the brood of chickens we had at home were properly taken care of. Nnamdi and I fed them dried maize from our farm. We took special care of the chickens that laid eggs; we prepared special places for them to complete the egg laying and hatching process. Once the eggs were hatched, we supplied plenty of food to the young ones to hasten their growth. We developed a peculiar whistling tune used to alert the chickens that it was mealtime; every time we made the sound, they would come running from all directions to where we were and we would litter the ground with maize while they ate. My mother always made it a point of duty to periodically prepare a chicken meal for the whole family to ensure that protein deficiency did not set in.

We supplemented the food we produced with the relief materials that my father occasionally brought home, like stockfish, stadit milk and corn-meal, which were periodically given out in his office as remuneration. All these measures helped my family and indeed many other families in Nnewi avoid *kwashiorkor*.

At my mother's maternity home, pregnant women attended antenatal and post-natal clinics. She lectured the women every Monday on what type of food they should give to their children to avoid *kwashiorkor*. You could tell by looking at some of the kids, with their yellowish-colored cheeks and puffy feet, that the dreaded disease had come. The pain on the faces of the women carrying such kids told the whole story. Essentially, the kids were being condemned to death because food was scarce. A refugee family from Onitsha that lived close to our house captured the totality of what the Biafran war and hunger turned people into. We used to go there to play with the rest of the kids and it was always a sight to behold every time they got ready to eat. Father, mother and kids would be struggling to get their fair share. Their father, a light-complexioned man, was already teetering on the edge of *kwashiorkor*. You could tell that he must once have been a very good-looking man, but the effect of this dreaded ailment had given him a frail look that was no longer appealing. He always struggled with the kids to get his own share of food and never worried about whether the kids were getting enough to eat themselves. Again, it was survival of the fittest. As a result, the kids had no respect for him; they called him all kinds of derogatory names, like *agudo*, which literally meant someone who guzzled food. It was always a painful sight, and I wondered why they all felt compelled to eat from the same plate? I felt that he could easily be given his own food on a separate plate while the children ate from another. I do not know what became of that family after the war, but that man was a very fine organist; he always came to our house to play my father's organ while I would sit on the floor, listening to his beautiful rendition of the Biafran national anthem. He seemed to be in a different world whenever he played the organ: his eyes would come aglow while he moved his hands in rhythmic fashion, sometimes humming the song.

Even as the whole world seemed to be deserting Biafra during that war, there were some countries that had the courage to defy all conventional wisdom and stand by Biafra. God bless those nations: Gabon, Ivory Coast, Zambia, Haiti and others. I knew their names by heart because every morning when we prayed, my father would always ask God to be with them and give them the fortitude to continue to stand with the truth, even when it was not fashionable to do so. He always lambasted Egypt, Ian Smith and his Rhodesia, Russia and other nations he referred to as *ndi alakuba*. We memorized a psalm we read every morning and night: "*Chineke, buso ndi n'ebuso anyi ogu, ogu, buso ndi n'ebuso anyi agha, jide ota na ota ukwu bilie inyere anyi aka...*"(God fight those that fight us, take up a big bow and arrow and arise and help us...) I thanked the nations that supported Biafra because nations like Gabon took it upon themselves to airlift starving Biafran children to Gabon to feed them, clothe them and give them succor. Even those on the brink of death, slowed down by *kwashiorkor*, came back from Gabon at the end of the war looking hale and hearty. I recall that I did not know then that Gabon was in Africa—I used to think that it was overseas, or *obodo oyibo*, and I actually envied those starving children who were being sent over there! Those were the thoughts of an eight—or nine-year-old who was not quite in tune with the gravity of the holocaust in Biafra. Meanwhile, our heroes were dying on the warfront and quick funerals were being held for those whose bodies could be retrieved by Biafran soldiers.

6

Asaba Massacre Hits Home

Boy Scout was one of our favorite pastimes during the war. I was in the Boy Scout with Nnamdi and Charles. Even though Nnamdi was too young to understand what was being done, he always went with us and sometimes just played at the St. Mary's field while we had our meetings. I still remember some of our fellow Scouters, like Chigozie Ibekwe, Felix Aghamelu, Arinze Umobi, Benji Umobi, Ifeanyi Obi, Ekeyekwu Obi (I think) and, of course, our Scout master, who later became a priest after the war.

We spent time during Boy Scout meetings learning new things like how to dodge air raids and how to hoist the Biafran flag, tie the rope and then gallantly salute it in military style. That was always a proud moment and a definite source of pleasure for me. The flag ceremony evoked a certain feeling of patriotism and love for nation in me, and I sense that it was the same for other kids judging from how serious they usually took the exercise. Every time we conducted the flag ceremony, I always felt like a junior Biafran soldier.

We also learned the significance of the colors of the flag, which were red, black and green, as well as a rising sun in the middle. The red symbolized the blood of Biafran civilians killed in northern Nigeria during the pogroms of 1966; the black signified mourning for those killed in the same pogrom. The green color symbolized prosperity, while the sun signified the dawn of a new day, free from oppression. If this symbolism was meant to sustain the fighting spirit in Biafrans and to constantly remind them of why the war was being fought, it achieved its goal. I knew this because every time we recited the significance of the colors of the flag, I always felt an instant surge of rage. I would remember stories of how angry mobs in northern Nigeria, armed with dangerous weapons like clubs, axes, poison arrows and machetes, rampaged through the streets in 1966, clubbing and axing easterners to death and raping their women folk while the army and the police, who were supposed to protect the easterners, stood idly, enjoying the carnage. This anger was not just peculiar to me, it was the same with most of the kids in my Boy Scout troop. We began to feel that scouting was definitely a stepping-stone into joining the Biafran program called "Boys Company."

Boys Company was a youth program put together by the Biafran army for young boys between ages eight and fourteen. According to story, the boys were trained in intelligence gathering for Biafrans. A typical intelligence-gathering operation entailed dressing up one of the boys in tattered clothes to look like an orphan. The boy then casually but discreetly strolled behind enemy lines, making a mental note of enemy location, troop concentration and size of armament. After successful reconnaissance, the boy would return to Biafra and give Biafran troops the information with which attacks on the federal troops were planned. If captured, the boy would claim to be an orphan trying to find his way back to Biafra. The Biafran army figured, according to the story, that the federal troops would not kill the boys, so the younger the boys were, the better.

I envied the Biafran boys who were said to be in the Boys Company. There was this particular boy from my village called George Orji. He was said to be in the Boys Company and usually followed his uncle, Arthur Ngwube, a Biafran army officer, to the warfront. We heard that George had a complete army uniform and had actually seen action on many occasions! I never personally saw him in uniform, but we kept hearing all these stories about his bravery, and we believed every bit of it. At a point, the story was that he owned a helmet, which he got directly from the head of a dead Nigerian soldier! Like most kids then, I always wished I could be in his shoes. In 1973, I got into the same secondary school that he was already in; he was two classes ahead of me. He was nicknamed Gary Cooper. Each time I saw him, all those incredulous stories about the war, and his supposed exploits, would come back to mind. I never got to ask him about those stories, but how I wish I had. I do not know where he is now. All the same, throughout our secondary school days, I regarded him with some reverence, just because of the war stories.

As much as I marveled at the "feats" supposedly performed by the Boys Company, I sometimes wondered to myself that Nigerian soldiers would be foolish if they did not become suspicious of the young boys after seeing several of them successively in their theaters of operation, all dressed in tattered clothes and claiming to be orphans. But at that time, we believed a lot of stereotypes about the Hausa soldiers. They were said to be devoid of analytical abilities and were not intelligent. Some of the stereotypes were captured in a song by the Voice of Biafran Revolution, and went thus:

Ndi Awusa bu mmakakwu
Ndi Awusa bu mmakakwu
Uche efi Awusa, Uche efi Awusa

meaning:

The Hausas are not mentally astute
The Hausas are not mentally astute
They have the minds of Hausa cows; they have the minds of Hausa cows...

These stereotypes sometimes beclouded my vision as a young boy, however, I still felt that no matter how dumb the soldiers were, they would someday discover that the boys allegedly presenting themselves as orphans were really Biafran spies and would start killing them. I also felt that the stories we were hearing about the exploits of the Boys Company might just be too good to be true.

This was the same type of question that I had about another Biafran military outfit that was called the Biafran Organization of Freedom

Fighters (BOFF). The program was said to be for an elite group of brave Biafrans. They operated in the warfront without guns because they got extensive training in judo and knew how to subdue and kill people with bare hands. Their greatest weapon was the element of surprise; they would swoop into enemy territory, conduct guerrilla warfare and one by one, kill off the soldiers and then bring back intelligence into Biafra. One of my paternal cousins was thought to be in the BOFF. I have never asked him if the story was true, but we all admired him every time he came back from where he was stationed. We would sit around and admire the hands with which he supposedly killed the enemy. I was close to him when I was in Nigeria and I still wonder why I never mustered the gumption to ask him about all those incredible stories about the BOFF and their war exploits. Maybe, in a way, I wanted the story to remain the truth in my mind, and I did not want to spoil my fantasy by asking and being told that the whole story was not true.

Regardless of the fact that the stories we were hearing about all these outfits in Biafra sometimes sounded unbelievable, we were encouraged; they continued to buoy up our hopes that, somehow, Biafra would prevail. We continued to do our best in the Boy Scout; I hoped it would help me fulfill my dream of getting into the so-called Boys Company. I not only wanted to be seen as brave, but I also wanted to genuinely contribute to the war effort. I saw Boy Scout as my best opportunity to achieve my goal.

One day, after a very entertaining Boy Scout session, Nnamdi and I returned home while singing one of our favorite scout songs:

A scout is a friend to all
And a brother to every other scout.
No matter to what country, class or creed,
The other may belong.

I always felt a certain amount of ambivalence in this song; on one hand, Biafrans were being maltreated by federal troops, but the scout song seemed to be telling us that in spite of that, we still had to be brothers with them. I could not understand it, but I sang the song anyway.

As I stepped into our compound with Nnamdi in tow, I immediately noticed that there were several people gathered in our house, inside the parlor. When we came closer, we could hear someone sobbing and the people were trying to console her; it was my mother. I was alarmed! As a kid, I failed to fully recognize that just as any other human being, my mother was susceptible to occasional sadness and pain. Therefore, any time I saw her looking sad or expressing pain, I always felt like the whole world had come crashing down on me.

On this day, she was not just sad, she was crying uncontrollably and reeling on the floor. Not too long before the war started, she had gone through that type of grief in Lagos when her brother, Mr. Lloyd Gwam, the Nigerian Director of National Archives, suddenly died in Ibadan. This was sometime in 1965 or so. That day, I was sure that my mother was going to die also; it was very painful to watch her crying uncontrollably.

As a result of this, when I saw her crying, with people trying to console her, I knew that something terrible had happened and my heart skipped. My first thought was that Fidelis had been killed. At the verandah stood Ezengozi; he was not crying but was just gazing into the compound without saying a word to anybody. I went up to him first and asked what the problem was, since I could not immediately get access to my mother; Ezengozi did not say a word. After trying for several more times and getting nowhere, I proceeded to ask others. I then heard that my mother's father and several other relatives had been summarily shot by federal troops in Asaba. The news hit me like a thunderbolt; it was like a nightmare and I was hoping to wake up. Incidentally, just a little while before that day, my mother had said that her first priority after the war would be to go to Asaba and reunite with her father and others. Now her hopes would never be realized. I was exceedingly embittered by this latest atrocity by the Nigerian soldiers. I hated the Nigerian head of state, Yakubu Gowon; I hated his commander, Theophilus Danjuma and I hated the so-called black scorpion, Brigadier Benjamin Adekunle, who I later met in person in 1982. I hated these men not because of anything I know they did in particular, but because as a little boy in Biafra, those were the names we always heard of as the core people driving the war and causing the killing of Biafrans. As a young Christian boy, I wondered why God would let such calamity befall us; I felt that all the prayers we offered to God every morning amounted to nothing since he would not protect us from the evil fangs of the enemy. I was feeling bad without even hearing the full story.

It turned out that even though we were just hearing about the tragedy then, it actually occurred several months before that day. According to story, when the Nigerian troops entered Asaba, they rounded up as many natives as they could, accused them of collusion with Biafra and then lined them up and started shooting! Some men were shot right in front of their wives, and then the women were made to bury their husbands. It was gruesome! The following were the people we lost in that massacre: my grandfather, G.W. Gwam, also called Insurmountable, his brother, called Gwam *nta*, my uncle Gibson Gwam and many relatives. That was too much to bear in one swoop. I pitied my father because he had his hands full; he did not know how to start consoling a woman who had just lost her father, brother, uncle and several other close relatives. His prayer that night was the most passionate I have ever heard someone offer; it was full of questions to God, why, why, why Lord? Why have you forsaken your children, Lord, why? He blamed Britain in his prayers for aiding and abetting the federal troops; he blamed Czechoslovakia; he blamed Egypt and all those supporting the Nigerian troops and causing this suffering on Biafrans. I had never seen my father that emotional before then, I saw him as a pillar of strength, one who was unflinching under any circumstance. On that day, I saw the other side of him; he was working very hard to guard against breaking down; he tried very hard to summon some inner strength to support my mother. It was very painful for me; I simply despised Yakubu Gowon and abhorred his lieutenants.

Uncle Lloyd Gwam—Nigeria's former Director of National Archives

*1965-My grandfather, **G.W. Gwam** (second from left sitting, killed during the Asaba massacre), His brother, **Gwam nta** (fourth from left sitting, killed during the massacre), my mother (far right sitting), Aunt Maria Edozien (standing second from left), Uncle J.D. Gwam (standing third from left)*

Asaba was one of the towns that suffered immensely at the hands of the Nigerian troops during the Biafran war. When the war started, it was part of the midwestern region and the governor, Col. David Ejoor, had previously declared that in the event of a war, the midwestern region would be neutral. However, many young men from Asaba gallantly fought on the side of Biafra and many Asaba indigenes took sanctuary in various places inside Biafra. There were many elderly people, including my grandfather, who did not see any reason to leave Asaba—after all, in conventional wars, women, children and the elderly were not targeted. This belief turned out to be a major mistake, because when the federal troops entered Asaba, they conducted a holocaust of unimaginable proportion; they killed as many people as they could find, regardless of their ages. With that, the Nigerian war broke all the rules of conventional warfare. It started with the senseless killings of defenseless Easterners in 1966 and was followed by the Asaba massacre. It was compounded with the starvation of many innocent people.

At the end of the war, in Asaba, it was clear that a gap existed; there were many women and children, but young men and elderly men were substantially reduced in number. The remaining young men formed social groups, such as the Asaba *Ndu ofu* or "new life" society, and through socialization, they tried to begin to put the horrible events of the war behind them and begin life anew.

The Asaba massacre is a tragedy that should not be swept under the carpet; it must be addressed somehow to avoid a repeat of such a horrible scenario in Nigeria and around the world. The human rights commission under Justice Chukwudifu Oputa, which was established by Nigeria's president to look into cases of human rights violation, has taken testimonies from those who witnessed the massacre or were directly affected by it. Testimonies alone would not prevent such occurrences in future. The perpetrators need to be identified and sanctioned in one form or the other, to show that Nigeria will not tolerate such sadistic acts in the future.

A chance meeting with Brigadier Benjamin Adekunle—the Black Scorpion.

I heard so much about Brigadier Adekunle during the war. My understanding then was that he was the Nigerian commander in charge of the Third Marine Commando. He was said to be a tough, no nonsense army commander who was so brave that he ate bravado for lunch and washed it down with ruthlessness! For that reason, I conjured up an image of him as probably six feet tall and very charismatic. I surmised that those qualities caused people to fear him and respect his commands during the war. This image quickly evaporated when I met the Brigadier in 1982. I had just returned from the United States where I, along with my friend and roommate at the University of Nigeria, Mike Ukoha (Micky Jagger), had gone to prepare our final year thesis projects. Because of flight arrangements, we had to have a layover in Lagos before heading back to Enugu to commence classes. This must have been sometime in October or November of 1982. My sister, Ijeoma, who had just returned with her family from the United States that very period, suggested that Micky and I stay in the house of a friend of hers, called Betty, for the night. We were to resume our journey the next day. Micky and I were given the address, so we went, and luckily, Betty was on hand to receive us; our baggage was taken to one of the rooms.

Micky and I went to Surulere to see a friend of mine, but by the time we came back, our boxes, which had hitherto been sent up to the room upstairs, were now stacked against one another in the foyer. As we stood looking around and wondering what happened, a slim built man of no more than about five feet, seven inches, alighted from the stairs, followed by Betty. He had a very stern look on his face; even when we said "good evening" he did not respond, so I stepped back. Then I heard Betty saying something to him in the Yoruba dialect, which I did not quite grasp, but I understood the part about "Brigadier, aburo Ije ni," which means, "Brigadier, this is Ije's younger brother." Ije is my sister and Betty's friend. It seemed as though that statement made the magic, because right after that, his countenance softened and he invited Micky and me to his study. As we were going upstairs in that gigantic mansion, I gingerly took in the splendor of the decorations in the rooms we were bypassing. On the wall of one of his living rooms hung a color picture of him in ceremonial military regalia; there was also a picture of a black scorpion hanging on the wall. In his study, he formally introduced himself as Brigadier Adekunle, and in my exuberance I asked him: "Are you the Adekunle of the Nigerian War?" It was as if a bomb had exploded; he thundered back in response, "Yes, I am. What did they tell you I did?" I spent the next twenty minutes or so trying to tell him that no one had said anything, but that I heard a lot about him during the war as a little boy. Again, he turned the tables on me, aggressively asking what I heard about him. It took a lot of rhetorical gerrymandering on my part before he finally gave me a break. Apparently, Micky had never even heard of him before and Micky is about two years older than I am! I concluded that Brigadier Adekunle is exceedingly sensitive about all the stories people bandied about how he prosecuted the war and his supposed ruthlessness in uprooting anyone that stood between him and his goals. That sensitivity must have triggered his reaction when I asked if he was Adekunle; it was tantamount to pushing his button.

When he had calmed down a little, he hurried downstairs, and came up with two plates of porridge and spoons; he gave Micky and I a plate each. After the obvious badgering we had just received, I was not sure if the food was given to us in good faith. I wanted to say no thanks, but to avoid another round of questioning from him I subdued my feelings and ate slowly, meanwhile wondering silently if that was the proverbial last supper!

During subsequent visits to his house in the company of my sister to see Betty, we met his other wife, Jumoke. In these instances, he seemed very pleasant, even making jokes. You could still sense the aura of authority around him; he was even called Brigadier in his own house and he definitely issued orders like the brigadier he was.

What surprised me most about Adekunle was that he was not as tall as I had expected. Neither could he be described as charismatic; I kept wondering how he managed to project all the bravery and commanding personality we heard about during the war. This is the same thought I had about the Biafran army commander, Col. JOG Achuzia, when I heard that he was only about 5' 6" tall and yet was able to effect all the heroics that were attributed to him during the Biafran War.

7

Conscription into the Biafran Army

There came a time when the Biafran authorities resorted to the conscription of young men to make up for the shortfall in the number of soldiers on the warfront. Morale had become low; adults who used to be upbeat about Biafra's chances of withstanding aggression and even repelling Nigeria's onslaught no longer talked in terms of winning the war; they now talked more about the war ending. Young men no longer enlisted in the army of their own volition and were therefore conscripted. I always felt bad watching as Biafran soldiers sometimes beat the men if they tried to resist going along with them. I felt that it was wrong for the Biafran army to harm citizens in the name of conscription; after all, the war was being fought to protest Nigeria's injustice, callousness and cruelty against Biafrans. Injustice by Biafrans on Biafrans was therefore unacceptable to me. What I may have failed to recognize at the time was that if such drastic and sometimes draconian measures had not been taken, very soon, not many young men would be available to fight the war, and the only alternative would be the unconditional surrender of Biafrans. Judging from the way I felt then, I would not have entertained the thought of surrendering to Nigeria. When I ponder the whole situation today, I can almost understand why the soldiers took the actions they did, however, some of them went overboard. Beating the men and sometimes inflicting very serious injuries on them because they resisted conscription was a case of soldiers overstepping the bounds of their authority. They probably had orders from their commanders to simply bring in more men for enlistment by any means necessary, so they did what they felt worked best.

The issue of Biafrans manhandling fellow Biafrans was the major reason why, during the course of the war, my onetime war hero, Col. JOG Achuzia of the Biafran command, turned into a villain in my eyes! At first, he was touted as a major force in the Biafran war theater, who was sent by his Excellency, Col. Odumegwu Ojukwu, to any front where things became tough. He was said to have been able to soften the enemy through superior tactical maneuvers wherever he went, and we loved it. Later, the story about Col. Achuzia changed; we started hearing that he did not tolerate any modicum of dissent within his ranks, no matter how minor, and would ruthlessly shoot any Biafran soldier who failed to obey his orders! We continued to wonder what the families of Achuzia's alleged victims were told as the cause of death of their relatives? People started wondering if he had an agenda different from those of other Biafran commanders. We were particularly intrigued that other soldiers made no attempt to remove him; after all, he was only one man. When the discussion about why other soldiers failed to remove him came up, some people said that he had extrasensory powers that enabled him to uncover any impending mutiny and would use any means necessary, including summary execution, to quell it. All these stories bothered me; I felt that if they were true, then he no longer acted in the interest of Biafra. The jury is still out on whether what he purportedly did was right, given the circumstances at the time. Some feel that he had to take such drastic actions in order to bring unruly soldiers in line with army rules and regulations. His supporters feel that war exigencies demanded unflinching support and loyalty. They argued that whatever means used to achieve loyalty and support was fine. They also felt that for him to continue to command the loyalty of his troops, he had to instill fear. In my opinion, if he really did those things, he went to the extreme! It is one thing to shoot a soldier because he took part in or masterminded a mutiny; it is another thing to shoot the soldier just because of a suspicion that he is harboring intent to mutiny. Manhandling fellow Biafrans during conscription (to me) fell along the same line as what Col. Achuzia purportedly did, and I did not like it at all.

At this time in Biafra, conscription was not limited to men who were clearly of army age, young boys of fifteen and sixteen were conscripted; even big fourteen-year-olds were sometimes taken away. Young boys no longer had the freedom to roam the villages, because they would immediately be taken away and sent to war. A typical conscription exercise consisted of three or four soldiers, armed to the teeth, suddenly swooping onto the village. They would then disperse and while some went from house to house in search of men of army age, others would hang outside the compounds, hoping to catch those attempting to escape. For young men, the best way to evade conscription was simply to avoid being seen by the soldiers, otherwise they would chase the person and then threaten him with orders like, "*If you move, I go shoot.*" Of course, the young men would choose not to be shot, simply give up and would be taken away.

We were sometimes lookouts for men who simply did not wish to join the army. We would be playing outside and once we saw Biafran soldiers, we would immediately send some pre-arranged signal to the men to hide away. Initially, the soldiers just came in, glanced around and then left, but as hostilities increased on the warfronts, soldiers intensified their conscription efforts; they would come into a compound and even search the bedrooms and attics, or *uko*. Some would even stake out houses of those they suspect of harboring men of army age, and would pounce whenever the person showed up.

Conscription gave some of our women folk a lot of advantage over their "cowardly" husbands who were afraid to go to war. During domestic arguments between husbands and wives, all the woman had to do was to threaten to call the soldiers to come and conscript the man and the argument would be settled immediately. These men suddenly became subservient to their wives just so they would not be delivered into the hands of the army. Some of them prepared permanent hiding places in the attics of their houses and spent a great deal of time in those places on days that conscriptors hovered around.

After a while, it seemed like the conscription exercise degenerated into a malicious quest; quarreling families would call the army on opposing families if they had men of army age; it became a potent way of settling vendetta!

At one time, a cousin of mine, a barrister, was conscripted on his wedding day, right at the wedding reception! Guests were already seated and the bride and groom were on the high table when Biafran soldiers swooped down on the place. The reception was being held in an open field, with canopies built with palm fronds. The soldiers simply went to the high table, took the groom, who was resplendently dressed in his wedding suit, and left. The chaos that ensued was unbelievable; the bride was dazed and confused and was crying while the guests huddled in groups, discussing the development. I believe that some influential people were dispatched to the training depot where my cousin was taken to, because after about two hours or so he came back. The wedding was completed in a hurry and all the pomp and pageantry originally planned for that day were never consummated.

Conscription had far-reaching ramifications on the young nation of Biafra; husbands were forcefully taken away without adequate time to say goodbye to their wives or children. Young men were taken away without saying goodbye to their parents, brothers and sisters. Sometimes, families would not even know that their loved ones had been conscripted; they would only find out when they failed to show up in their respective houses in the evening. There was a training depot at the location where soldiers of the Eleventh Division were stationed in Nkwo Nnewi. Families went there to verify that their relatives had been conscripted. Because there was no time to give conscripted men adequate military training before being sent off to war, sheer fear immobilized them on the warfront the first time they faced the enemy. According to stories, on the sound of gunfire, some would try to scurry back to the rear in which case, they could face court martial for cowardice!

A relative of mine we called Ogbonta told a story, after the war, of how he was conscripted and sent to the warfront. He was scared and confused the first time he was in the warfront, so at the first opportunity, he climbed a tree just to keep out of sight. At night, he fell asleep on top of the tree and fell down. That fall inflicted serious injuries on him; he was sent to the rear and so never really made much contribution to the war effort. Stories like this abound; some soldiers were said to have inflicted injuries on themselves just to avoid going to the warfront and facing the enemy. This must not be held against them, because no one without adequate training and preparation of the mind can just go to the warfront and become a hero. Some could not stand the zoom clang of war machines, the booming sound of heavy artillery and, of course, the gruesome sight of men dying. Also, some of the soldiers went for several days without food. Now, how could someone be physically and emotionally fit to fight on empty stomach? The soldiers who first enlisted at the outset of the war had more and better military training and psychological preparation before being sent off to war. They were properly fed, too. This may have accounted for the morale boosting gains Biafra made at the beginning.

Conscription and its attendant effects hit closer to me when Biafran soldiers took my elementary three schoolteacher away. Before then, I had thought that teachers were essential personnel in Biafra and so were exempt from the service. I was shocked when the news was broken to me. The day after he was taken away, we came to class only to be informed that our teacher had been conscripted, and we would now be merged with another elementary three class located in the compound of the Egwuatu family in the same village. We grudgingly obliged but preffered our teacher; he was ahead of his time and was always proactive in his teachings. The class we joined was just about beginning to study fractions, even though my own class had already perfected fractions under our erstwhile teacher.

Our new class was overflowing with kids; it seemed like we were more than 100 children and the classroom had a tunnel-like rectangular shape.

Those of us who sat in the back rarely heard what the two female teachers said. The result was that during class, kids in the back would be chattering and the teachers did not seem to care. That always worried me because I felt that we were not learning much in that class.

8

Emma Goes to War

The main objective of conscription in Biafra was to continually replenish our fighting forces on the warfronts. After a while, that method became less efficient, if not ineffective. Men of army age had learned to hide and keep away from the prying eyes of conscriptors and their informants. When conscription was originally instituted, any time the soldiers came to the villages they picked up many young men. But at this point, they would gallivant all day in the villages and finally leave empty handed, or with just a few men. Sometimes, out of frustration, they would pick up kids who were obviously underage only to let them go the next day or so. Because of this, the soldiers had to devise another way to lure young men out. They started staging military displays, which attracted many people to Nkwo Nnewi. During the displays, the soldiers furtively moved about and rounded up young men for enlistment. After a little while, they also hit a dead end with this tactic; people had found out the real reason behind the military displays and stopped showing up, forcing the soldiers to look for yet another way to reach their elusive targets.

I think that the army must have met with village elders because, very soon, it was decreed that each village was to nominate a certain number of men for enlistment; it was called *igu ami*. Village chiefs were to ensure that the task was accomplished. Each nominee became the representative of the clan that nominated him. The problem was that there was not enough time to train these new recruits. Some were trained for three or four days and then sent off to war; of course this increased their vulnerability in the theater of operations where they were deployed.

My clan, Okpunoeze, just like other clans, was divided into wards, and each ward was made up of close and extended family members. As the head of our extended family and coupled with the fact that he was overly patriotic and willing to do what it took to get Biafra to win, my father felt responsible for producing a nominee for our clan. My brother Emmanuel was a fifteen-year-old boy at the time. When the war started, he was a class-two student at the Ika Grammar School, Agbor, in the Midwest. It was bewildering to us when my father suddenly announced that he was about to nominate his fifteen-year-old son as Ward-22 representative. Up until that moment, it never occurred to any one of us that he would even be considered for enlistment into the army; he was simply too young (although he was an above-average boy in height). I felt that my father could easily have pointed to Fidelis as our contribution to the Biafran cause. My mother could not believe this; she pointed out that there were many men of army age in Okpunoeze who would be better suited, psychologically and mentally, to be on the warfronts than Emmanuel.

She tried to protest this move but saw that she was not getting anywhere. Also, since Emmanuel was not showing any reluctance to joining the army, it was even more difficult for my mother to make her case that he was simply not mature enough to go. My mother was not only concerned by his age but she also worried that sending him out without adequate training was tantamount to homicide, and she was determined to do something about it. She acted quickly and my aunt, Mrs. Maria Edozien, who was a military nurse in Owerri, helped facilitate Emmanuel's enlistment at Owerri as a military police officer. This move provided the opportunity for him to be trained for a whopping one month!

During the training in Owerri, he was given a rifle for target shooting. Of course, as a young boy who had not handled a gun before and who was not mentally prepared for what he was facing, he misfired in the target range. This incident nearly ended the life of the staff sergeant in charge. One would expect that any punishment he was to be given would be tempered with mercy, given his age and inexperience, this did not happen, and here is how he recalls it: "...When I fired the rifle, the muzzle velocity pushed me back and I fell down and accidentally discharged another round in the process, nearly ending the life of the staff sergeant...I had the worst day of my life as I was properly beaten and sent to the guardroom for three horrible days..."

He continued to serve Biafra as a military police officer. The only time he visited Nnewi during his service, we noticed that he had lost a lot of weight but seemed to have quickly grown taller and more matured for his age; we were very proud of him. During that visit, he was dressed in full military uniform, and what impressed me most was that, given the circumstance surrounding his enlistment, he was not bitter at all or angry at anyone. He never argued about going to the war, because he felt that it was the right thing to do. He went to the war out of patriotism and because of his sensitivities towards the suffering masses. He had seen *kwashiorkor* killing Biafran folks; he had seen many dying of heartbreak and he had seen mothers burying their children and sons, and he was determined to help end the suffering.

Born in Jos, Emmanuel started from the early days of his life to develop a knack for adventurism. As a little boy, he once cut open the grate-like material covering the speaker of the radio in our house. When asked why he did that and before his punishment could be pronounced, he said he wanted to see the man who was talking inside the radio. He also had a very funny and likable personality which usually endeared him to the hearts of people he came in contact with; no wonder his report cards at Ika Grammar school in those days always had the comment, "Emmanuel is very amiable."

He was initially deployed as a military police officer, however, when the federal troops cut off his troop, thereby denying them access to food and reinforcement, it was every soldier to himself and the fight for survival began. As he remembers it, "I stayed on till we were cut off by the federal troops, because of the sudden pull out of one of the Biafran divisions stationed at the town of Ikot Ekpene. Major Sylvanus Okeke of the blessed memory was a commander in that division. We all embarked upon Operation Open Corridor, trying to fight our way through the blockade. Some women who came there initially on *afia attack* to buy foodstuffs and go back into the Biafran enclave were killed during this operation. Soldiers of the Nigerian Third Marine Commando had a field day besieging us at the town of Uzoakoli. We were almost out of munitions and most of our soldiers had not tasted food for days. Many lost their lives during that siege."

Back home in Nnewi, we had lost all contact with Emmanuel, even as we no longer heard from Fidelis. When we did not hear from Emmanuel after a while, my father actually regretted his decision to compel him to go into the army. He talked about how other well-heeled people in Biafra sent their children overseas while other people's children were on the warfront, fighting and dying.

This would later become an issue in Biafra; people wondered why relatives of highly placed Biafran officials, who were clearly of army age, evaded the war. Some ended up overseas while those who remained in Biafra moved about freely, often with army exemption passes signed by highly placed commanders. Even as a little boy, I perceived that as a form of injustice; I felt that if Biafra's seeming indomitable spirit was to endure, that form of favoritism should be eschewed in its entirety. This issue became a very sensitive one for me; every time I saw someone who looked like he was of army age but was still in the rear, I felt troubled by it. I felt that if two of my brothers, who were clearly not of army age, enlisted and were on the warfront, then others should be on the front as well. I began to detest those called "stragglers." Stragglers were soldiers who left the warfront and came to the rear, in the villages, gallivanting from one place to the other. Most people did not have patience with them; they were seen as frittering away the time they should be using to engage the enemy head-on. The army was not patient with this caliber of soldiers either. They took time to locate and punish them. I found it amazing that in most instances, these so-called stragglers told more stories about war heroics than those who were actually fighting the war. Some told stories about how they nearly caught Col. Yakubu Gowon with their bare hands!

There was this particular guy in my village. He was in the Biafran army but it seemed like he was always home during the weekends. What struck me most was that his uniform was always very clean, well starched and ironed and he never ran out of incredible stories to tell about the war, the warfront and the casualties Nigeria was sustaining. I wondered whether the warfront he told us about was the same one that other soldiers went to. My vision of a warfront then was of a muddy, bushy and dirty place; I expected that a soldier coming straight from there would at least look dirty, but you would never see him dirty. His stories not withstanding, I saw him as a straggler.

I was also not very convinced that the presence of the Biafran army division stationed in Nnewi, called Eleventh Division, under colonel Amadi, was necessary. From what I could observe as a child, Nnewi was not immediately threatened, and yet, every time one passed by Eleventh Division, at the Maria Regina High School, you would see an endless number of soldiers milling around. I felt that they could be put to better use if deployed to the real warfronts, like Onitsha or Abagana sector. Some of the soldiers did things that heightened my uneasiness with them. They started rounding up children to go and fetch water for them. My problem with that was not the fact that they got kids to fetch water for them—it was the least one could do to help the war effort. I was appalled that they did it with force and intimidation, as if the intimidation we were getting from Nigeria was not enough. All the same, my spirit of patriotism always rose above any misgivings I had against any set of people in Biafra. I was still very proud of Biafra and I was very proud of Fidelis, Emmanuel and other numerous gallant Biafran soldiers, fighting and dying, but checkmating Nigeria's attempt to wipe out a whole race.

A peculiar phenomenon developed amongst soldiers in Biafra at this time. Soldiers began losing part of their hearing as a result of close proximity to artillery guns. For some soldiers, the hearing loss was temporary and corrected itself after a couple of days or weeks, but for some, it seemed to linger for quite a long time. One thing that puzzled me was the transformation this syndrome seemed to have on some of the soldiers; they lost their ability to speak the Igbo dialect! They all spoke broken English in very loud voices, and I always wondered about that. We called these soldiers *ati ngbo*, and to the kids this became a testimony of a soldier's bravado; we mimicked them, trying to look brave, because the thinking was that a soldier who was so close to the artillery gun that he lost his hearing must have participated in the war and was not a straggler.

I remember Paul, a boy that helped aunt Mamaocha in her cooking and food selling business. Five months after Paul was conscripted into the Biafran army, he came back to Nnewi in full military uniform with a helmet to match. He looked exactly to us like the real deal—the brave Biafran soldier who had fought on the warfront. When we tried to approach him as he entered our compound, he was frantically pointing to his ears and then in a very loud voice said, "*Wey mama ocha, make she come pay me my money.*" It was unmistakably *ati ngbo*. To the kids, Paul was now accomplished and the transformation was complete; he no longer spoke the Nnewi dialect for which he was noted when he was working for Mamaocha. He now spoke in authoritative broken English. It was hilarious! I was surprised because throughout the time that Paul worked for Mamaocha, I never heard him speak a single word of the English language but now he spoke the broken English authoritatively. Of course Mamaocha quickly paid Paul the money he was asking for, both out of fear and partly out of admiration that Paul had become a complete Biafran soldier. He was now *ndi nke anyi*, our people.

One day, Biafran soldiers sprung an element of surprise on us; they furtively slipped through our gate so the kids did not have enough lead-time to warn the adults ahead of time that conscriptors had come. We were all sitting inside our family *Ozobi* playing the game of *ncholokoto*, or mancala. As soon as they entered the compound, one of them bellowed, "*Make nobody move,*" and in response we all froze where we were. Once they secured our undivided attention, they quietly made their way to where Ezengozi was sitting, grabbed him by the hand and slowly started leading him away. Ezengozi did not resist but he did not seem to be going along willingly either, so they dragged him along, one soldier on the right hand and another on the left. He looked very calm and said nothing, as though he knew that this day would come. Someone must have alerted my mother in her maternity, because before the soldiers could walk as far as the pathway that led from our house to St. Mary's Church, a distance of less than 100 yards, there she was, running after the soldiers. She was resplendent in her nursing uniform with her cap to match. We all ran after her and in my mind, I hoped that the soldiers would give Ezengozi a break once they found out that his sister was helping save lives in Biafra. When we caught up with the soldiers, one of them just casually glanced backwards and caught a glimpse of my mother but then turned around and continued, meanwhile tugging at Ezengozi to move along faster. My mum then introduced herself to them, but I noticed that they did not even seem to care because they never looked backwards; even Ezengozi just continued on as though he never heard my mother speaking. At this juncture, my mother burst out crying while imploring the soldiers to release my uncle. She called their attention to the fact that two of her sons were already in the army and that she had lost her father, uncle and brother in the war already. She told them that taking away his brother was like attempting to wipe out a whole family. The stern-faced soldiers never paid any attention to what she was saying; they just dragged Ezengozi along. After following the soldiers for a while and seeing that they were not giving in to our pleas, we all turned around and sorrowfully went back to the house. Ezengozi was very much loved in my family and we knew that he was going to be missed. We sat around in our parlor, pondering what the next step would be. Of course we prayed and asked God to be with him wherever they would take him to.

I am not quite sure what happened, but Ezengozi later returned to our house in the evening and said he was released unconditionally; in my mind, that was divine intervention, because my mother had already started praying and asking God to bring her brother back.

9

Nnewi Is Bombed

Starvation was not the only means that Nigeria used to attempt to break the spirit of Biafra and cow her into submission. When the war started, it was believed that the rules of conventional warfare would apply and hence, air raids and military assaults would only be targeted at army formations. As things progressed, it became clear that Nigeria was determined to break all the rules of conventional warfare; they bombed civilians with reckless abandon and the havoc they were causing in civilian enclaves was utterly gruesome! The testament to the carnage they left in their wake could be seen all over Biafra—maimed children, men and women with missing body parts, destroyed residential buildings, cratered highways with skeletal remains littered all over them and the constant smell of death in the air.

A man's life was literally turned upside down in the town of Aba. On that day, the town was being bombed and strafed by Nigerian jet fighters and bombers and civilians were running all over the place for cover. A bomb which was dropped by one of the aircrafts landed very close to the man's house; it first drilled into the ground before exploding. The explosion unearthed a large quantity of soil and so the man, who was running for cover at the time, was buried alive with only parts of his body showing! After the air raid, other survivors discovered what had happened and subsequently rescued him. Half of his body was burnt and his skin had literally peeled off from his waist to his head, giving him a pinkish look on the upper half of his body. He was later brought back to Nnewi and, as anyone would imagine, was a sorrowful sight to behold. As if conscious of his physical appearance, which was sometimes very frightening to children, he used a hat to cover his head. Every time he went by our house, I could not help but wonder how horrible the experience must have been for him, yet those were some of the harsh realities of the war. Many Biafran civilians lost their lives during air raids; it was not clear at first whether the civilians were being purposely targeted, but as the mayhem continued unabated, it became clear that it was a deliberate policy by Nigeria aimed at exterminating Biafra. Air raid survivors were all over Biafra; they were willing to tell anyone the story of the atrocities they witnessed and endured. The trauma was so severe that some of them suffered panic attacks any time they heard sounds that remotely resembled that of an aircraft. It was disappointing that the world community allowed the destruction of lives of such a magnitude to continue without serious intervention. We continued to suffer in Biafra, wondering what the world was doing about it, not knowing that international politics was precluding even those who sympathized with us from coming to our aid.

I am not sure how this story got to Biafra, or who the source was, but it was said that since Nigeria did not have enough qualified pilots, but were bent on bombing civilian targets, they naturally went looking for mercenary pilots, who would have no problems with targeting civilians. Eventually, they found accomplices in Egyptian pilots. The ruthless and heartless pilots started doing the bidding of their Nigerian employers, bombing everything in sight, dispossessing mothers of their children and robbing children of their parents through deadly air assaults.

While we were hearing about the atrocities the Egyptian pilots were visiting on civilians all over Biafra, Nnewi was yet to witness an air raid. Some said that Nnewi was not bombed because the enemy planes could not locate the town; others said that *Edo*, or the deity, in Nnewi, protected the town from air raids. Some even suggested that all the native doctors in Nnewi came together and put a powerful protective charm over the town and that every time the warplanes went by Nnewi all they saw was a body of water. I do not know about the adults, but the kids believed all these stories completely and so felt somewhat safe and immune from Nigeria's air assaults. We had no reason to dispute the stories because the airplanes still had not shown up in Nnewi, but that was about to change.

One day, late in the morning, just after market women had left for the market and the rest of us were going about our business, we suddenly heard the sound of an aircraft in the distance. The sound would sometimes get louder, as though the aircraft was coming towards our direction, and then start receding gradually into the distance. We could tell that it was not the usual aircraft that brought food to Biafra, because the relief flights were conducted at night. They also flew at a very high altitude and had a peculiar lazy, drone-like sort of sound. The menacing sound we were hearing this time was definitely coming from a fast aircraft, flying at a lower altitude. As we huddled around to ponder what all that meant, some of the refugees amongst us who had witnessed air raids elsewhere in Biafra confirmed that what they were hearing was reminiscent of the war planes that harassed, bombed and strafed their locations elsewhere in Biafra. Not sure what to make of all this, we just stood around listening intently as the sound of the plane continued to increase and ebb interchangeably. Then the unthinkable happened; a loud sound of what seemed like an explosion could be heard in the distance; this was followed by secondary but more subdued sounds of exploding ordnance. The secondary explosions seemed to be coming in succession and the whole thing sounded like a choreographed sound display. Before this time, even though we had not experienced an air raid in my town, we had learnt all the necessary steps to take in case one materialized. We were supposed to dive for cover on the ground or run into the bush and take cover. If caught unawares, while walking along a road, we were to stand still and the planes would mistake us for "inanimate objects."

Once the explosions started, instinct took over and we did exactly what we had been taught; we all rushed out into the adjacent farmland and lay as motionless as possible on the ground. It was somewhat amusing watching children, adults and the elderly, scurrying for cover inside the bush. The seriousness and fear on everyone's faces, however, was a constant reminder that it was not fun and games; it was serious business, and taking the wrong course of action could mean instant death through hellfire spewed forth by the Egyptian pilots. This sound of exploding ordnance continued for quite some time but after what seemed like forever, a deafening silence, occasionally punctuated by the sound of chirping birds, descended on the whole place. Slowly, and one after the other, we started crawling out of our hiding places. Some were making the sign of the cross on their chests, while others were openly saying things like, *Chukwu dalu*, meaning, thank God; little did we know that our thankfulness was premature. One peculiar thing about that whole episode was that while we were all scurrying for cover, my grandmother never moved from where she sat in the verandah of her house. She continued to do this throughout all the air raids we experienced. Till this day, I have been unable to tell if she did that out of sheer bravery or if she just felt that, at her age, death was no longer frightening. She later passed away peacefully in 1977, seven years after the end of the war.

When aunt Mamaocha came back from the market later that day, she said that the planes hit their target; it was *ilo ekwusigo* in Oraifite and environs. Oraifite is a town next to Nnewi and had one of the few tarred roads in the area at the time, and that road was called *ilo ekwusigo*. No one could decipher the logic behind bombing a stretch of tarred road and some buildings around it; but some surmised that they were probably trying to isolate some areas and preclude transportation of troops or food from one part to the other. It seemed like the pilots had finally found the route to Nnewi and from that day on, everyone realized that "air raid" had come close to home and Nnewi's invincibility may just have started unraveling. Some people began to panic on the grounds that it might not be long before the pilots bombed our town, but some native doctors still boasted openly that they had things under control. They were adamant that any time the pilots flew over Nnewi, what they saw was a body of water and nothing more. They would amusingly say: "Even though we know that they (the federal troops and Egyptian pilots) have the intelligence of cows (*uche efi awusa*), we do not think that they would be foolish enough to start bombing a body of water, because that is what they see when they fly over Nnewi."

One of the native doctors, who was also a proponent of the fact that Nnewi was protected, used to say that his "supernatural powers" came from many years of training in India. Sometimes, while seated with people in his compound, he would suddenly shout, "I am coming," and then run to the back of his house. He would later return with several items that could only be purchased from a store like Kingsway Supermarket. He would then say that he had ordered those things from India and that when his order was ready, the Indians signaled him through the "thin air" and told him where to pick up his order. This display was always very amusing to me, but as a little boy who did not know any better, I sort of believed. After all, at that time, we all thought that India was the repository of supernatural powers. It did not surprise me, therefore, when he continued to reinforce the idea that his group of native doctors put a protective charm over Nnewi. I felt that if any one could perform that type of feat, it would be an Indian-trained person.

Not too long after the *ilo ekwusigo* air raid, Nnewi was found. I am not sure what time of the day it was, but on that day, the morning sun was already up and casting a very long shadow on the ground. I was in my grandmother's house, which was adjacent to my father's house, and suddenly a deafening sound enveloped Nnewi. Everyone, with the exception of my grandmother, rushed outside, and before we could do much, two very fast-moving aircrafts were zooming past overhead at a very low altitude. We could see them clearly, prompting my uncle, Godwin, to exclaim that if we had a double barrel gun handy, we could down the airplanes. The planes zoomed past our house and then, in the distance, they unleashed mayhem; the sound was as thunderous as it was deafening; my heart was in my mouth and pounded faster than I had ever experienced all my life. At that time, we had all taken up our places of cover, wondering who the recipients of Nigeria's latest round of atrocious madness were. This harassment continued, with sounds of explosions that seemed to be increasing progressively over time. I lay where I was and the thought of the man who was buried alive in Aba by air raid came into my mind. I wondered if this was our turn and if so, who would be the survivors this time. Nobody spoke a word and every time one looked at the faces of everybody else seeking refuge in that farmland, one saw the faces of a people frightened beyond belief; a people who had realized that life could be taken away at any time, thanks to the warplanes. No one knew what to expect. Even those who had witnessed air raids before were as frightened as those of us new to the experience. The aircrafts dominated the skies, flying back and forth and unloading their arsenal on civilians in the distance while we waited for what seemed like an eternity, hoping we would not be found. Some people swore that they could see the faces of the pilots in the aircrafts smiling as they did their evil duty; the planes were that low. It seemed as though their plan was to run through Nnewi, unload some of their payload, turn around and start all over again, unchallenged.

Prior to that air raid, Nkwo Nnewi market, which was in an open location, had been relocated to another area, around one of the villages we called Otolo. That area seemed more secure because of the ubiquitous presence of trees in it. I remember that when I first went to that new location; I noticed that the dense cover of the tree leaves made it seem like evening time in the market all the time. You could hardly see the sky. It turned out that when the place was cleared, the tree branches and leaves were deliberately left intact while the ground brushes were cleared completely. The branches and leaves therefore provided round-the-clock shade over the area. People could freely display their wares and walk around without fear of being detected by the enemy from the skies. During this bombing run, however, the warplanes bombed the market. Shrapnel hit my cousin, Chika, who was at the market on that day. She spent some time at the Ikedife Hospital, in Otolo Nnewi, and still carries the scars to this day. It dawned on us, after that air raid, that the belief that the deity protected Nnewi no longer held water. There and then, we knew that the entire story about pilots seeing a body of water when they flew over Nnewi was balderdash! It was every man to himself and God for us all.

As people pondered what had happened during that air raid, a very disturbing rumor emerged: some felt that, given the location of that market and the dense cover of vegetation over it, there was no way the enemy could have found it easily unless they got help from Biafrans. The suggestion was that we might have saboteurs amongst us who informed the enemy of the location of the market. I kept wondering why turncoats existed in Biafra (if they did), a thought that has continued in my mind to this day. The turncoats were called saboteurs; they were said to have sold their allegiance to the federal troops and given out our war secrets and troop locations. They revealed operational and tactical information to the enemy and made Biafra vulnerable. Some people still feel that Biafra's defeat was partly because of the role *sabos* (as they were called) played in the war. Nobody ever substantiated the allegation about the fact that saboteurs may have given out information that led to the bombing of Nnewi market, but that thought never left my mind.

After that air raid, as days passed, we started attempting to put the ugly experience behind us. We were hoping that it would be a one-time experience, but we were wrong. Several days later, another air raid occurred. It seemed as though the federal side was gloating over the fact that they finally found Nnewi, the home of the leader of Biafra, Col. Odumegwu-Ojukwu. I was headed to the spring with Ezengozi, Edith and Uchenna to fetch water when the aircrafts zoomed past overhead. Of course, the road to that spring was always busy, with people going with their water containers and others coming from the spring with their water cans or buckets balanced on their heads. Once it became clear to everyone that it was another air raid, some people quickly threw down what they were carrying and ran into the adjacent farmland for cover. Some stood still where they were (as we were told to do) because there was not enough time to run into the bush for cover. Then all hell broke loose; deafening sounds of explosion filled the atmosphere. Because we were close to the descent into the hill that led to the spring, the echo of the sound bouncing off the hill filled the air. Before long, balls of black clouds or smoke surrounded the aircrafts, which had now gone up higher in altitude into the atmosphere. At first, we thought that the black balls of smoke were also airplanes so many of the people seeking refuge in the farmland were crying and saying that the aircrafts had come for the final assault to exterminate Nnewi from the face of the earth. The balls of smoke must have numbered more than twenty around the two aircrafts. As we prayed silently and waited, the balls of smoke gradually started dissipating. No one could fathom what was happening; from our hiding places, we continued to exchange confused glances. When the aircrafts seemed to move out of the area, the deafening sound we were hearing would subside, but then, when they showed up again, it would resume with a vengeance. This continued until, finally, the planes seemed to leave the area. After a short wait, we all started crawling out of our hiding places while those who froze in their tracks unfroze themselves and started moving again; one could see bewildered and panic-stricken faces all over. Some people, who threw down their bucketful of water when the nightmare began, decided to go home without water. Ezengozi convinced us to go down and fetch the water anyway, since we were already close to the spring. On the way, we continued to discuss the latest round of air raids and how it differed starkly from the one we witnessed before.

When we got home from the stream, we were told that the deafening sound we heard when the aircrafts came was the sound of anti-aircraft fire. Biafran soldiers were firing at the warplanes. It turned out that after the first air raid in Nnewi, Biafran authorities installed several anti-aircraft guns in strategic locations in Nnewi. They installed some very near to our house in a place called *Eke Eze*. The proximity of the guns to us explained why the sound was devastatingly deafening. During that air raid, because of the intensity of the anti-aircraft fire, the warplanes could not dominate our air space the way they did during the previous raid. They could not fly at low altitude as they did before and they were not able to find any targets.

When people found out what had happened, many went to *Eke Eze*, where the anti-aircraft guns and the gunners were stationed, to congratulate them. Some families cooked for the soldiers and for a moment, it seemed as though morale was beefed up once again within civilian ranks in Nnewi. Some of the morale-boosting songs we used to sing started resurfacing again: "*Biafra kunie, buso Nigeria agha...*" Meaning, "Biafra, get up and fight Nigeria..."

The air raid we experienced in Nnewi paled in comparison with what was happening in other parts of Biafra, such as Umuahia, Aba, Owerri and others. In those places, the pilots routinely went into densely populated areas and markets and bombed them, leaving a trail of destruction in their wake, destruction that included burnt, charred and decapitated human remains. Buildings were also reduced to rubbles so that those who managed to survive the raids became instant refugees in their own towns.

When we were instructed, at the outset of the war, to freeze in our tracks if caught unawares during an air raid, I thought that it was a full proof way of avoiding detection. Now I know better—it was not. I realized the folly of what we were doing when I first flew in an airplane in 1978, during my second year at the University of Nigeria. That day, as the commercial aircraft I was flying in started its descent into Ikeja Airport, I could clearly see people, cars, roads, trees and other things. I then realized that the fighters and bombers that came on bombing missions in Biafra saw us; it dawned on me that it was only providence that helped those of us who survived the air raids. This kept me wondering how many people may have died at the hands of the Egyptian pilots because they stood still in the open during air raids.

Nnewi was visited a few more times by the "fighters and bombers," but at those times the anti-aircraft guns installed in *Eke Eze* did not let them do much. Every time the Russian-made MIGs came calling, the deafening sounds of fire from the anti-aircraft guns precluded them from completing their missions of harassing civilians. We were always in a constant state of alert, ready to run out and dive for cover. It was unnerving, especially for a little boy in his formative years. The psychological and traumatic effect from that experience is unimaginable and may sometimes still linger in some people.

The experience we had with the air raids brought about some measures of uneasiness in our house and, I am sure, throughout Nnewi. It was an experience we were not accustomed to, so any time we heard sounds akin to that of an aircraft, flying overhead, we took measures to get out of harm's way.

On this night, there was a dull but sustained sound in the atmosphere; Mamaocha surmised that it was *ndi ilo*, the enemy. Before long, intermittent flashes of light followed the sound from the atmosphere. Mamaocha said she recalled that it was said at the market that *ndi ilo* now had a way of taking pictures of the lay of the land and then coming back later to embark on bombing raids with pinpoint accuracy. Once Mamaocha said this, my mother's stepmother, *mama nnukwu*, concurred with her. Before we knew it, we had packed up our mats and blankets and moved to the open space under the mango tree in front of our house. The logic was that if they came to bomb our house later, we would all be under the mango tree.

We stayed and stayed and the sound continued, with the flashes of light following in succession. Charles, Obiageli, Nnamdi and I passed time telling stories that my uncle Ezengozi had thought us. "*Inum anwupu, nwukwudo mbe*" he would say, which was an Asaba phrase that simply meant, "My story starts with the turtle…" With that, we would tell all kinds of tales mainly concerned with the turtle. Most stories that Ezengozi taught us always ended with a moral: "Do not be greedy" or "Be a loyal friend." I recall that Ezengozi was the very first person who told us the story of the animal farm. He was my most favorite uncle; he was funny, smart, witty and down to earth. At his prodding, during the war, even though I was just in elementary three, I memorized my times table from two to twelve and have not forgotten a word of it to this day. When he passed away in 1977, while a part three student of Political Science at the University of Ibadan in

Nigeria, I was devastated. Ezengozi left a void that no one has ever been able to fill.

As the night wore on, the sound and flashes of light started abating and later stopped altogether. When we reached a consensus that it was finally over, we packed our things and went back into the house. I felt, in my mind, that the sound we were hearing was the rumbling of thunder and the flash of light was lightning, but at this time, we had all become paranoid about air raids and I believe that no amount of convincing would have dissuaded Mamaocha or Mama *nnukwu*. As we stepped into the compound, we noticed that while we were all outside trying to hide from *ndi ilo*, my father was still in the parlor with the lamp, reading, oblivious to what we were doing. Again, I wondered if he just felt that there was no cause for alarm or that he was invincible. Maybe he simply thought we were overreacting and did not want to spoil our "fun," and so ignored our panic. I will never know why he did that.

Mamaocha always brought home exciting and morale-boosting stories about the exploits of Biafran soldiers during the war. She usually went to nkwo Nnewi market on a daily basis, and I do not remember if she went to sell something or not, but for a while during the war, she operated a small *buka* in our compound, where she sold *nni oka* and *ofe ogbono*, which is fufu made from corn and ogbono soup. One thing became peculiar about those trips to nkwo market: every time she came back, she would have a positive story about Biafra's performance on the warfront. Her story usually started with, "*ndi nke anyi sulu ndi Nigeria akwu tata...*" ("Our people unleashed mayhem on Nigerians today...") and that would set the stage for her story. I remember one day, during the first few months of the war. Mamaocha came home from the market and as she walked through the gate, she shouted, "Halleluiah!" The sound attracted everyone's attention and before long we were gathered around her to hear the latest news about Biafra. She said that the Biafran soldiers had crossed the Midwest and had gone as far as the town of Ore; they were said to be poised to capture Lagos. Everyone was elated; they attributed the success to the fact that Biafra had well-trained army commanders who wasted no time in putting their expertise to work. I was as happy as everyone else, but I kept wondering what would happen if Biafran soldiers took Lagos. Would we be able to go back and live in Lagos? I wondered. Nonetheless, we continued to celebrate the feat, but it turned out that we started celebrating too early.

One day, my father came home and announced that Biafra had completely retreated from Ore and had lost all the grounds gained! We heard all types of rumors as to why the mission to capture Lagos failed. It was a major set back for Biafra, but Mamaocha never relented in her optimism and positive stories. She would tell how Biafran *ogbunigwe* was used to kill a whole battalion of federal troops in a particular sector. *Ogbunigwe* was the Biafran-made mine that was said to wreak havoc when properly targeted. She would tell these stories with so much seriousness and conviction that one would think that she had witnessed them firsthand. It surprised me however, that some of the grownups in the family referred to her as "radio without battery" and did not seem to pay too much attention to her stories. That annoyed me, because I wanted to believe all her stories as true, since they generally boosted my morale. I always found myself thinking of the people that called her "radio without battery" as pessimists who did not realize that their attitude would get Biafra nowhere. The war had already ended when I realized that some of the stories were mere propaganda that market women usually peddled in the market arena without knowing it. Some of the stories would start out as correct, but as they "traveled" from person to person, they became adulterated in favor of Biafra. The versions that Mamaocha usually brought home were the best pro-Biafran versions. She was very patriotic and therefore her optimistic stories became her contribution to the war effort. There was a radio broadcaster called Okoko Ndem in Biafra. He was so good with pro-Biafran news reports that every time I listened to his accounts on the status of the war effort my optimism about Biafra's ability to withstand aggression waxed stronger. He would talk about how our gallant soldiers killed a battalion of Nigerian soldiers, took their weapons, clothes and shoes and even ate their food! The pro-Biafran stories were Okoko Ndem's contribution to the war. Some people helped by going to the warfront and putting their lives on the line, others helped by trading behind enemy lines and bringing food to help feed the starving masses, while Mamaocha helped by peddling pro-Biafran stories, unaware that some of them were mere propaganda. That was the least she could do and she did it very well. Up till this day, I think that Mamaocha believed those stories, and that was why she was telling them.

Our bomb shelter in Nnewi

As a result of the wave of air raids Nnewi was witnessing, my father decided to construct a bomb shelter to lessen our chances of being hit. Behind our house was a parcel of land with a very big *iroko* tree in the middle. The enormous branches of the tree provided an unbelievable canopy over the land. Standing on that parcel of land one could hardly see the skies. As a result of the cover provided by the *iroko* tree and other smaller trees, that land, which is now the permanent site of Uzoma Maternity Home, became my father's choice for the bomb shelter. When my family first came back from Lagos at the outset of the war, the *iroko* tree used to be a resting place for bats that we called *usu kangwu* and some villagers had my father's permission to set their bat traps on the tree. The traps consisted of strings laid out in nuts dangling from the tree. Whenever the bats flew into the strings, they were trapped and later retrieved by the bat hunters. I do not now remember what they did with the bats because I am tempted to say that people do not eat bats, at least not anyone that I am aware of.

The choice of that parcel of land for the bomb shelter, pleased everyone. Even without a bomb shelter, the trees provided a lot of cover; it was doubtful that the airplanes would ever think of it as a viable target for their mayhem. My father arranged with some men to come and construct a bomb shelter. On the appointed day, the men all gathered under the *iroko* tree and work began; while some were cutting down palm trees, the others were excavating the ground. They needed the palm tree trunks for the roof of the shelter. This was not a one-day activity; it took several days of work with intermittent stoppages any time it was suspected that an enemy plane was in the neighborhood. Also, the men dispersed into the neighboring bushes anytime their lookout signaled that army conscriptors were coming. This delayed the work, but they did manage to finish after a couple of days and finally we had our very own bomb shelter. It was built by excavating the earth to a depth of about six feet or so. The trunks of the palm trees they cut down were laid over the excavated pit close to each other horizontally. Several layers of clay soil were then placed over the tree trunks and consolidated with homemade tampers. An opening was created on one end of the pit and steps were carved out of the earth leading down into the pit from that end. For a while this bunker gave us a great sense of security, because it was said that enemy bombs would not be able to penetrate it.

I was happy that we had the shelter, but a few things bothered me: it was always very dark inside it, and when it rained, even though we had some corrugated metal covering over the entrance, water still seeped into it making it muddy and unpleasant to stay in. The bunker was short lived, however, because one day, my uncle found a big and poisonous snake inside it! That day, it became clear that the dark and cool crevice had become a breeding ground for all sorts of dangerous creatures. When my father heard about the snake, he immediately decided that we were no longer going to use the bunker. His thinking was that we had no way of preventing the proliferation of the dangerous creatures inside it. He did not want anyone to be bitten by some poisonous snake inside the bunker; that would be an irony—losing one's life in an attempt to save it from air raid. As for me, I felt that one had no chances of surviving if confronted by a poisonous snake in such a confined and dark enclosure as the bunker. It was therefore better to fall back to what we had done before: run for cover in the event of an air raid. I do not even think that we ever got to use it for shelter during an actual air raid, because I cannot remember any air raid during the short life of the bunker. That bunker was later cleared and back-filled and it became one of those things that was never really consummated. I do not know how widespread the construction of bunkers was in Biafra, or in Nnewi for that matter, but I never really heard anyone say that they were constructing a bunker. Of course, it may have been one of those things people kept secret for fear of being sabotaged.

I must confess, though, that I now wonder what good that the bunker would have done us had the warplanes found it as a target. For one thing, the thickness of soil used to backfill it, in retrospect, was no greater than two feet. When this is added to the thickness of the tree trunks, the total cover would come to about three and a half to four feet. Also, the earth was not properly consolidated because there were no mechanical compactors to achieve a better compaction. For all these reasons, I believe that a bomb targeted at the shelter would easily have penetrated the roof and buried us all alive.

10

Voice of Biafran Revolution

At the outset of the Biafran war in 1967, all of the eastern region was awash with the spirit of patriotism. People were willing to do whatever it would take to win the war; even music was used as a medium for condemning the aggression of the federal troops against the young nation of Biafra. It was also used to heap praises on Biafran soldiers, who were seen as not only smart, but exceedingly daring and brave.

Like many other Anglican churches, St. Mary's Church in Nnewi had her very own choir; it was made up of men and women who had lived in Nnewi most of their lives. Even though they were often lightheartedly referred to as *amulu n'uno, bi n'uno*, or born in the village and living in the village, they nonetheless made a great choral outfit. However, when the famed musicologist Sam Ojukwu, no relation of Col. Ojukwu, returned to Nnewi at the inception of the war, he decided to upgrade St. Mary's choir. By dint of either his vision or serendipity, he gave the choir the mythical status it enjoyed in Biafra throughout the war.

He started the upgrade by changing the name of the choir to Voice of Biafran Revolution (VOBR); this was intended to depict the exigencies of the time. He had a small panel van on which he boldly displayed the name "Voice of Biafran Revolution" and his grand idea was that the new choral outfit would sing songs in French, English and Igbo. Later on, having noticed that many members of the choir were not secondary school educated and as such were having problems pronouncing some English and French words in his songs, he went to the Anglican Girls Secondary School in Nnewi and recruited some girls.

With this injection of fresh blood into the choir, a new breed of singers emerged. Ijeoma, who was also in the secondary school at Anglican Girls, joined the choir also. It did not take long before the group became recognized as Biafra's singing mouthpiece; they were invited to special occasions to sing for Biafran dignitaries and people of their ilk. They traveled around Biafra and entertained people with the various songs composed by Sam. I have always been a great lover of music, but initially, I thought that their show was an adult affair and so never went to watch them, even when they sang in public places close to our house. As a result of all this, I never appreciated the magnitude of the effect their songs were having on Biafrans. One day, that changed. The setting was inside St. Mary's Church; I do not remember what the occasion was, but the church was packed full with people. In those war days, it took very little to assemble a big crowd, since most were not working and so used extracurricular activities to pass time. The choir was seated on one end of the church, very close to the altar, and a grand piano was strategically positioned very close to them, near the permanent location of Chief Z. C. Obi's chair in the church. Chief Z. C. Obi was the former chairman of Igbo Union; he hailed from Uruagu Nnewi and was an ardent member of the St. Mary's Church. The atmosphere was filled with anticipation because the choir had developed a reputation for mesmerizing her audience and most people may have come that day to see things for themselves.

After a short time, Sam Ojukwu rose from where he was sitting and walked over to the piano; he pulled up a stool, sat down and comfortably positioned himself in front of it. He then motioned to his soloist to get into position; the soloist turned out to be a young man I later came to know as Ifeanyi Obi. Ifeanyi majestically strode up the steps that led up to the church altar and stopped midway; he then turned around and faced the congregation; you could have heard the sound of a pin drop on the concrete floor of the church because of the silence that ensued. He sat loosely on the altar rail, leaned back slightly and crossed his legs. Meanwhile, more silence. At that moment, the sound of the piano rang out; Sam Ojukwu was melodramatically plucking away at the white and black keys on the piano while swaying slightly from side to side in the manner of Stevie Wonder or Ray Charles. "*Nobody knows the trouble I've seen...*," Ifeanyi sang. The song itself was very appropriate for the time, because most Biafrans were still trying to get over the pogroms that had taken place in northern Nigeria in which many hadlost their parents, uncles and siblings. Even though Ifeanyi was singing without a microphone, his velvet voice caused a slight echo that bounced around the church, giving the performance an extraterrestrial feeling. The effect of Ifeanyi's song on the audience was immediately evident on their faces; many nodded their heads in obvious appreciation while others just starred in awe. After a while, he slowly rose from the altar rail, cast a sweeping but gentle glance at the audience from one side of the church to the other, as if to verify the genuineness of the captivating looks on their faces, and then continued his song. The polished nature of his act reminded me of the singers we used to watch in the movies at the Yaba College of Technology field in Lagos. In my mind, he looked as self-assured as any one of those singers, and the congregation loved it. At the end of it all, one could tell from the thunderous ovation he got from the audience that he had not disappointed them one bit. He took a bow and left the improvised stage. With that performance, the stage was set for the rest of the choral marvels that the VOBR unleashed.

Next came Margaret and Isaac Ngwube. They walked up the stage, stood opposite one another, and remained motionless for a moment. Meanwhile, the audience was wondering what they were about to do. Then, with Sam Ojukwu leading the tune on the piano, they started singing a French song. Many in the audience, like me, did not understand what they were saying, but it really did not matter, because they demonstrated what they were saying in pantomimic fashion. The whole thing captivated me so much so that I kept wishing that I had grown old enough to take the place of Isaac; I was actually developing an instant crush on Margaret, who was probably five or six years older than I was. Margaret was beautiful, elegant and graceful, and she moved about the stage with graceful ease, gesturing to her counterpart as the song required. Isaac was equally putting up an 'A' plus performance. At the end of the song, Sam Ojukwu said that the title of the song was "*Ne plues pas, Jeanette*"—"Don't cry, Janet." That day, the Voice of Biafran Revolution made a believer out of me with the various songs they sang. They sang other nationalistic and morale-boosting songs, like the one Sam introduced as "*Okotoko Nigeria*," meaning, "Big for Nothing Nigeria." Part of the song went thus:

Biafra kwenu—enyimba, Biafra Kwenu, enyimba
Ebe Chukwu n'edu anyi n'agha
Egwu adiro
Ndi awusa si na mmiri, shore battery alua oluya
Hasigodu n'enu ani, ogbunigwe eme nkeya
Nekene nu ka ndi agha Biafra si asu fa akwu
Okotoko Nigeria, Yo –o, kwelu n' ike adirozigi

meaning:

Biafra answer, *enyimba*, Biafra answer *enyimba*
Since the Lord is with us in this war
There is no fear
If Hausa tries to attack us through the sea, shore battery will be used
    to kill them
If they try to come by land, *ogbunigwe* will decimate them
Look at how Biafran soldiers are killing them.
Big for nothing Nigeria, yo-o, admit you have no more strength

Enyimba is a rallying war cry that the Igbo people used in the past; I do not know what the origin is, but mixed into this mellifluous but earthy song, the whole performance hit a nerve with the audience. By the time the song ended, people were cheering one another, smiling and laughing heartily. "*Okotoko Nigeria*" later became a popular phrase in Nnewi; every time the choir sang that song subsequently, the audience would join in, singing and nodding in appreciation. Sam Ojukwu therefore became a musical icon, very relevant in the scheme of things in the young Biafran nation. That day, their grande finale swept me off my feet, for right before our eyes, he motioned to six children, including Ida Ojukwu, who later became my very close friend; Ubaka Ojukwu, who also became my classmate and friend, and I think that Chiemeka Ileka was there also. There were three boys and three girls facing one another. Sam then started the tune and the whole church was agog; the choir was singing cheerfully, Sam Ojukwu was playing his piano heartily and the kids were dancing away. What impressed me the most was that even though the song was in French, the kids seemed to be singing along while dancing. Ida was the youngest of the dancers, but the ever-present smile on her beautiful face and the grace with which she glided effortlessly on the dance floor easily made her the favorite of the audience as well as my personal favorite. The song was called "L'armor" and I wondered if the kids had taken a crash course in French, or whether they were just mouthing the song, since they were doing it so well.

At the end of the song, Sam went up the stage and explained that the title of the song meant, "Love is Blind." After that, the kids bowed and took their leave while the whole congregation rose up in applause. I could not believe my eyes; I wondered how the kids secured such coveted positions in the VOBR and vowed to attempt to join. Later, Charles, Obiageli and I went and tried out for membership in the children's dancing troupe and were lucky that the three of us were chosen. With that, we became official members of the "elite" dancing troupe. My little brother, Nnamdi, was still too young to join. We went places with the VOBR and danced for many Biafran dignitaries. People have often asked how I know so much about the Biafran war given my age then; I have always responded that membership in the choral group was partially responsible, because we spent most of our time in the midst of older members of the group, listening to stories about what was happening in the war. These were some of the members of the dancing troupe as I remember them: Ubaka Ojukwu, Ida Ojukwu, Charles Edozien,

Chiemeka Ileka, Obiageli Edozien, Nnamdi Unigwe, Alfred Uzokwe, Edith Mbanugo (I think) and some kids that had the surname of Adibua. After we joined the group, membership was expanded to twelve instead of the traditional six. We opened performances for the Voice of Biafran Revolution with a five to six minute dance to the French song "L'armor." I loved it so much and will never forget a trip the VOBR made, all seated in the back of a lorry or *gwongworo.*

Sam Ojukwu had earlier told the group that we had been invited to sing for some members of the Biafran army in a neighboring town called Ozubulu, a few miles away from Nnewi. The kids were ecstatic; we cherished going along with the VOBR to do our dance and this invitation provided another opportunity for us to go and display our dancing talents, or so we felt. This invitation was very special, because we were going to be singing and dancing in a military environment. Some of us had not been that up and close to very active Biafran soldiers, so we longingly waited for the day. Meanwhile, I was already imagining what to expect—a group of gallant soldiers all resplendently dressed in camouflage and the trademark beret of the Biafran commandos. Of course, I had to do first things first— I made sure that my clothes were washed ahead of time and laid out in one corner of my mother's room.

On the appointed day, Ijeoma, Charles, Obiageli and I folded our outing clothes into our bags and began the 15-minute walk to the St. Mary's Church compound. The evening sun was already beginning to set and was casting a reddish-blue haze over the horizon when we arrived at the church compound. Other members of the choral group were also beginning to arrive, one after the other. We gathered in front of the pastor's house; the kids huddled on one side, while the older people huddled on another, discussing issues I never really bothered listening to because my mind was full of anticipation as to what we were going to see. As minutes turned into hours, the anticipation, which had almost built up to feverish proportions within me, gradually started dissipating; it became clear that we were in no hurry to depart. Just as it was beginning to get dark, a lorry arrived. At this time, Ijeoma took us to the side of the church and we dressed. Because of scarcity of clothes, we treated our outing clothes with great care. We usually wore our casual clothes to the gathering place and only changed into our dancing clothes when we were ready to depart for the dancing venue. As we were emerging from where we went to dress up, Sam Ojukwu drove in. He had a small chat with the driver of the lorry and summoned the members of the singing troupe. After last minute discussions and instructions, we all boarded the open lorry, while Sam took some of the people in his car, and the journey to Ozubulu began.

When we arrived at the place, it was already very dark and we were ushered into a building that looked like a student hostel. At strategic corners were gas lamps positioned to throw as much light as possible on every corner of the hall. We all headed to the end of the hall where the members of the choral group started taking their normal positions. Members of the Biafran armed forces started coming in and to my amazement, what I had imagined was not exactly what I saw. Some of the young men coming into the hall were limping, some walked with the aid of crutches, others were missing some body parts, like arms or legs, and some wore bandages over their heads. I could not hide my alarm. Further inquiry revealed that we actually came to sing for wounded Biafran soldiers to beef up their spirits. I saw the gesture as a worthy cause, but because most stories we heard about Biafran soldiers concerned their bravery, it took a while for me to soak in the fact that Biafran soldiers were sustaining injuries of unimaginable proportions. Before long, the hall was filled to capacity and became very warm and uncomfortable. The performance was scheduled in the night, just like most occasions in Biafra, for fear of detection by enemy warplanes.

We performed that night as usual but I left that hall with a very heavy heart. The sight of Biafran soldiers with all manner of physically incapacitating injuries was too much for me to bear. I vividly remember one soldier whose head was completely bandaged, including his eyes; I kept wondering what type of injury he sustained that would necessitate wrapping his whole head with bandage. He, however, did not seem to have sustained a broken spirit, because, even though he could not see us, after each performance he seemed to clap the most. Such was the spirit of most Biafrans, willing to make the ultimate sacrifice in the defense of their fatherland.

From that day on, I no longer believed all the war propaganda I heard. We returned home to Nnewi in the wee hours of the night and instead of the feeling of elation I usually had after our performances, I was down. Every time I fell asleep, the image of what I saw reappeared and I would be jolted awake! I wondered how many more soldiers had been wounded and immobilized and scattered all over Biafra while their families were thinking that they were still on the warfronts. Also, I wondered how many must have died all because of a war they had not caused.

The visit to that military depot or hospital got me thinking about my brothers, Fidelis and Emmanuel. Could it be that they were in a military hospital somewhere in Biafra without our knowledge? If so, could it be that they had sustained injuries as terrible as the ones we had just seen? Could it even be that they were no longer alive? All these terrible thoughts continued to circle in my mind and every time I tried to push them out, they came back again with a vengeance. I began to feel that if this was the price of the war, it was not worth it.

The clanging and twanging of war machines, the rat-tat-tat sound of the rifles of the men of the infantry, periodically punctuated by the boom sound of heavy artillery, could always be heard in Nnewi. The sound emanated from Onitsha, where Biafran soldiers were fighting and dying by the hundreds to protect the rest of us in the Biafran enclave, which had become reduced substantially. When the federal troops initially entered the town of Onitsha, and we started hearing the sound of gunfire and exploding ordnance, we were under the illusion that it meant that the Biafran troops were routing the enemy. Our visit to Ozubulu changed my outlook. From then on, every time I heard the sound of war machines, my heart would sink and I would wonder how many more Biafrans were going down.

11

His Excellency, General Odumegwu Ojukwu

My father, in no small measure, influenced the way I perceived the war. I got to hear his assessment of things on a daily basis; you could easily tell how he felt about the war in his prayers during our morning and evening devotions. We spent about one and a half hours every morning and evening praying, asking God to protect Biafra. He would mention the names of all of Ojukwu's advisers and ask God to guide them and give them the wisdom to continue to guide the young leader of the new nation. He always mentioned the name Brigadier Imo, as one of Ojukwu's advisers. I do not quite recall who the man was but my father spoke of him as a sage. Anytime it was my turn to pray, I would do exactly what he did, call out all those names, ask God to be with them and then end my prayer with, "God, guide the young leader of Biafra, who expended his father's considerable wealth selflessly, just to save his kindred from extermination." I got this notion from my father, who said that Col. Odumegwu Ojukwu used his father's money to buy all the initial resources, including the thirty-two rifles with which Biafra started her struggle for survival. To me then, Chukwuemeka Odumegwu Ojukwu was next to God.

There was this picture of him in one of the papers we had then: he was inspecting a guard of honor and the caption was something like "His Excellency taking salute from a gallant soldier." He looked very sharp in that picture and I was proud that he was my leader. His slightly burly looks gave him a very healthy appearance. That was a far cry from Gowon, who had a lean and hungry look, in my opinion. In my childish attempt to assure myself that Ojukwu was the greatest, I once asked Ezengozi the following question: "If Col. Ojukwu were to fight Gowon bare-handedly, who would win?" He simply said, ""All Ojukwu needs to do is to sit his 'big butt' on tiny Gowon and he would suffocate." I loved the answer that I got. It confirmed to me that Col. Odumegwu Ojukwu did not just look superior, he was indeed superior. I drew pictures of him and placed them in our *ozobi* for all to look at.

It was my reverence for Ojukwu that almost led me into doing something that would have put me at serious odds with my father. One day after choir practice with the VOBR, someone said that one Mr. Azuka Obi was going to wed at the St. Mary's Church. The man added that because Azuka Obi's mother was related to his Excellency, Ojukwu would be attending the wedding. I could not believe what I was hearing, and in my mind I resolved that I was going to do whatever it took to catch a glimpse of his Excellency for the first time ever. St Mary's Church was just a 15-minute walk away from my house and I was not about to let the opportunity pass. While pondering how to gatecrash the event, it dawned on me that the VOBR might actually be invited to the wedding, but before I could ask that question, the man who broke the news about the wedding said that for the sake of Ojukwu's security, the wedding was going to be at night and only a few senior members of VOBR were invited; my hope was dashed. I was devastated, yet optimistic. I was determined to catch a glimpse of the enigma that was Ojukwu, even though I knew the consequences of sneaking out of my house at night.

I started wondering who Azuka Obi was and how he may have been related to Ojukwu. I did not quite get the picture, but only heard that Azuka's mother was related to Ojukwu. I later found out that in our Boy Scout club, our troop leader, Ifeanyi Obi, who was also a singer with the Voice of Biafran Revolution, was Azuka Obi's brother, and therefore related to his Excellency! My regards for Ifeanyi skyrocketed, but when I told Ezengozi about Ifeanyi's relationship with Ojukwu, he said that they had

known all along. He added that it explained why Ifeanyi was not conscripted into the army like other boys his age and was still in the Boy Scouts
with us. Ezengozi jokingly added that Ifeanyi probably carried as much as
twenty passes, personally signed by his Excellency, to exempt him from
conscription. I cannot personally tell if Ifeanyi was old enough to go to war
or whether he had exemption passes, but he looked tall enough, and I
thought to myself that if Emmanuel could go to war, then Ifeanyi could
certainly be on the warfront also. But that was not peculiar to Ifeanyi,
because there were a lot of able-bodied men in the Voice of Biafran
Revolution who were old enough to serve in the war but did not. However,
they rendered their services to the nation through the songs, which were
morale boosters not just for people in Nnewi but also for Biafra as a whole.

On the evening of Azuka Obi's wedding, I could not do anything else
other than think about how to duck out of the house. I had one major constraint though; I was still afraid of the dark and was not ready to relegate
that thought to the background. Going along with Nnamdi at that time of
the night was out of the question because he slept in my mother's room. It
was said that his Excellency was going to arrive in a helicopter, and so every
time I heard a sound akin to that of a helicopter, my heart would miss a
beat. I continued this way until bedtime, when I drifted into a sleep filled
with episodes of being in the wedding and seeing his Excellency. For some
reason, I never followed up on whether that wedding took place or whether
Col. Ojukwu had come. Maybe I blocked that out of my mind just to minimize the pain of knowing that he had come so close and that I hadn't been
able to see him. It was good that I did not sneak out that night because I
would invariably have incurred the wrath of my father.

After this incident, we continued to hear that Col. Ojukwu periodically
visited a house right by St. Mary' Church. That was the family house of one
Mr. Douglas Ngwube, whom we were told was one of his advisers. One day,
we came to St Mary's field for our customary Boy Scout meeting only to
find out that the field was being dug up and "cultivated." Some people were
stacking palm fronds in one corner of the field while others were digging

holes, about one foot apart, on the field and "planting" the palm fronds. I could not understand the significance of this, but on further inquiry, I was told that Ojukwu would be visiting Douglas Ngwube and that his helicopter would be landing on the field adjacent to Douglas' house. The palm fronds were being "planted" to help camouflage the helicopter. Unlike some rumors in Biafra, which turn out to be false, the helicopter did land on the grounds of St. Mary's, but I did not see who came out of it and could not tell if Col. Ojukwu was in it or not. As soon as the helicopter landed, some soldiers hurriedly covered it with palm fronds.

I later met Douglas, in person, in 1984 or 1985, when he called to solicit my architectural services for the modification of a house he was building. He never knew that I had special respect for him. I felt that for Col. Ojukwu to pick him as an adviser, he must have been a very smart man. During that meeting, I continued to resist the urge to ask him questions about the war and what it felt like to be very close to his Excellency. My biggest constraint for not asking the question was that it was during the military era, when the discussion of Biafra was still done in hushed tones.

12

Ugonna Leaves for "Obodo Oyibo"

After the conscription of our teacher into the army and the merging of our class with other elementary three pupils, I got to meet a lot of new kids. Among them were Obiamaka Obi, Philip Ngwube, Ochiligwe Obi, Uzo Ike, Jane Epunam, Ofili Obi and Oliver Obi.

It was during this period that I met a boy of about my age called Ugonna Egemonye; we both sat at the back of the classroom. When I told him the village I was from and where our house was located, he told me, in turn, that his maternal grandfather, Mr. Ofueme (or *Onyenwugbo*, as he was aptly called) lived very close to our family, and that he visited them regularly. I do not remember how this happened but we struck up a deal where I would bring him some of the sweet tasting stadit milk that my father periodically brought home and he would in turn bring me a fruit we called *mbembe*. It was a small black fruit found in his locale, close to a neighboring town called Ichi. Our bartering flourished and strengthened our friendship, even though at times the scarcity of milk made it difficult for me to keep my own end of the bargain.

One day, to my utter amazement, Ugonna told me that his parents were living overseas, *obodo oyiwo*, as he called it. He had a very dense Nnewi accent and I always thought he was one of those we referred to as *amulu n'uno bi n'uno*. Nothing about him gave me any indication that his parents were living abroad. After overcoming my initial shock, I asked him why he was still in Biafra, particularly in Nnewi, suffering with the rest of us, if what he was saying was true. He simply responded that plans were afoot to send him and his two sisters abroad. When he said this, I could not help but wonder if he was insane to think that anyone could leave Biafra at a time when enemy soldiers surrounded us. I felt that his parents were merely telling them that they were coming to get them, just to make them feel better while surviving in Biafra. When I later talked to his maternal relatives, they confirmed that his parents were indeed living in London. I continued to wonder why they left them in Biafra in the first place, although I never asked him about it again.

As the war dragged on, Ugonna and I continued our trade by barter. I think that he later moved to his grandfather's house, along with his two sisters. There, they lived with their other cousins, Anyaegbunam and Ella Philips, and so they had a full compound. In that compound, there were many grapefruit trees, tangerines, oranges and cocoa fruits. We used to go there to play and, of course, help ourselves to the fruits.

One day in class, Ugonna casually said to me, "*Anyi n'eje obodo oyiwo*" meaning "We are going overseas." I could not believe what he was saying; it sounded like a joke, but the look on his face did not show any humor nor betray any underlying agenda. Again, I felt that it would be impossible to get out of Biafra. I sought more clarification from him and asked how they were going to get out. I believe he said that his father sent someone from *obodo oyiwo* to come and get them. I still felt it was the biggest joke ever told, but after that discussion we dropped the issue.

About a week or so later, after school, Ugonna invited me to his grandfather's house. During that visit, he told me that they were gathering things for their overseas journey; he climbed one of the grapefruit trees and started plucking grapefruits while his sisters were picking them up and placing them in what looked like an *akpa aji*, or woven sack. As this continued, I sat by myself, ruminating over this development and wondering what I would do if this eventually became a reality. After a while, I realized that it was getting late, so I took my leave and went home hoping to see him in class the next day to ask further questions about their exact day of departure. The next day, I woke up early, completed my morning chores quickly and left for school. When I got to the class, he was not on his chair, but I assumed that he was probably running late. As the day wore on, it became clear to me that he was not coming to school that day. I continued to wonder what had happened because he was not given to skipping school. At the end of the school day, I headed straight to their house and was shocked when his cousin, Anyaegbunam, told me that they had left for Britain. One part of me was happy for him but the other was filled with sorrow; I felt that I had once again been separated from another good friend of mine, an obvious replay of the scenario I had encountered in Lagos in 1966, when my friends and their families left Lagos to escape hostilities. As usual, I blamed the war.

That night, I had no respite. I wondered if he ever made it overseas, if he ever got to meet *ndi ocha* or *oyibo*. I wondered if he was going to be able to understand them when they spoke to him and I wondered what kind of friends he would find there. I wondered if he was ever going to learn how to walk fast like the *oyibo* people we always saw in movies when we were in Lagos. In those movies, it seemed like they were always walking fast and with hands in their pockets. It was much later that I understood that walking fast had a lot to do with the weather; no one ambles around in cold weather. With all these thoughts in my mind, I drifted into a restless sleep. I never heard from Ugonna again; but as days chugged along, I learned to exist without him and turned my attention elsewhere, to my cousins, Charles, Obiageli, Emeka and, of course, my little brother, Nnamdi.

When I visited the United States for the first time in 1979, I was amazed by the abundance of fruits like oranges, grapefruits and apples. I remember wondering why Ugonna went through the trouble of gathering grapefruits, tangerines and other fruits for their journey to Britain in 1969.

13

Myths in Biafra

During the Biafran war, there were many stories going around; some of them seemed incredulous, but because we could not easily determine their veracity, we simply accepted them as true.

B26 and Johnny the pilot

There was a story about a B26 aircraft that Biafra was said to have acquired during the war. According to the story, a brave and daring Israeli pilot called Johnny went on bombing missions deep inside enemy territory with that aircraft. We were told that on one occasion, during a bombing mission, one of the wings of the aircraft was shot out, but Johnny managed to fly the plane back to safety into Biafra. On another occasion, the aircraft was said to have been riddled with bullets and yet landed safely on Biafran soil. I have tried to verify whether a man called Johnny ever flew for Biafra during the war, but I always came up empty-handed. So far, all I could find was Carl Von Rosen. Carl helped with the training of Biafran pilots; he also flew some very small aircrafts they referred to as "Biafran babies." Also, Carl was not an Israeli.

Abiriba people and their supernatural abilities

At the outset of the war, the people of Biafra assessed their strength as well as factors that could help the nation withstand and repel Nigeria's onslaught. A story that took center stage was referred to as the "Abiriba story." Abiriba is an Igbo community that was said to be very brave, with war heroes who had overwhelmed their neighbors during wars in the past. The story continued that the reason why the Abiriba community had vanquished their enemies in wars was because of supernatural powers they possessed. They were said to be invisible in the battlefields; all the enemy saw were sword-wielding hands floating in the air and cutting down people's heads with abandon. Of course, it would be tough to fight invisible enemies.

As this story was repeatedly told in the eastern region at the outset of the war, the implication was that Abiriba people would be deployed to the warfronts and they would quickly take care of the enemy. People cited wars that they had fought and won in the past and how they used such powers to overwhelm and defeat their enemies. It was said that they were simply lying in wait for the order to charge the Nigerian troops. I do not know how much and in what capacity Biafra made use of the "supernatural" powers of the community, but as soon as the war started in earnest, we no longer heard anything about that.

Bowl of blood

One of the biggest problems that families encountered during the Biafran war was not knowing whether their loved ones had been killed. Things were not as advanced then to the point where soldiers were sent to notify parents or family members about the death of their beloved ones. As a result, it was always a case of guessing and rumors. Some people were rumored to have died but later returned to their families, and many that were said to be alive and well later turned out to have been killed.

A cousin of mine, Uche, lived with my family for some time during the war. After a while he left, and I do not remember where he went, but he was away for several months. Someone later came and told my family that Uche had been killed in the war along with his uncle, Tony. This generated a lot of sadness in the family; Uche was a jovial boy; with him and Ezengozi around, we had a lot of fun; we all played *ncholokoto* together, went to the farm and to the spring together. A few months after we heard the story, on a very sunny afternoon, Uche walked in. Nobody knew what to do. We were not sure if it was his ghost or real image. When he was later told what we heard, he jokingly said that had he known, he would have started acting strange when he walked into the compound, just to create the impression that he was a ghost. This type of scenario continued to play out in many places in Biafra. Even after the war, some people whose funeral rites had already been performed came back and others who were thought to be alive never returned.

The continued uncertainty about whether a soldier was still alive or not produced a story which I have been unable to verify. We heard that even as many families were wallowing in the uncertainty about the whereabouts of their loved ones, others were able to keep track of the status of their loved ones on the warfront. The story had it that on the day of the departure of their loved ones to join the army, they put water in a clean bowl and had the person dip his hands in the water before departing. The bowl with the water was then placed in a secure place in the house. The water would continue to be clear, as long as their loved one was alive but as soon as he was killed, the water would turn into blood. When I heard this, I wondered why there were no bowls kept for my brothers. I believed that if we had done what some others did, we would not be playing the guessing game of whether my brothers were alive or not.

14

Papa Dreams about Fidelis

At this time, we had not seen or heard from Fidelis or Emmanuel for a long time; my mother was worried sick and her anxiety level was always obvious every time she prayed. My father, on the other hand, always avoided showing how he felt, but I saw in him a man who was proud that he gave Biafra two of his sons in her defense. Sometimes, though, he would reiterate the fact that the bigwigs in Biafra had sent all their army-age children overseas, while the rest of us suffered. All the same, that did not dampen his patriotism. Every time we prayed, he would put my two brothers and all Biafran soldiers in the hands of God for protection. He would ask God to guide the nations that recognized us. Haiti was one of the nations that recognized Biafra. We were ecstatic that they recognized Biafra, but I did not realize that Haiti was just a tiny and poor nation that could do practically nothing for us. It was after the war, when we started studying the geography of nations, that I realized how poor Haiti was. Of course, they lent their moral support to Biafra, but in terms of resources, they could not help. That was part of Biafra's undoing. With the brave men, talents and homemade resources that Biafra had, if countries like Great Britain, which could have given us arms and money, had recognized us, Biafra, even with her smaller population, might have won the war.

Regardless of the shortfalls in nations that recognized us, the ingenuity of Biafrans probably saved us from total annihilation. One of the biggest feats Biafra performed was the development and implementation of the mine called *ogbunigwe* or "Ojukwu bucket" as the federal troops were said to have called it. It was not only homemade, but it was also made out of locally available materials. The name *ogbunigwe* which means "kills in large numbers," was derived from the fact that it usually killed the enemy in large numbers if properly targeted. We revered the Biafran scientists who developed the device, even though we did not know who they were then. We heard amazing stories about *ogbunigwe*; some said that no one Scientist in Biafra knew how to build it from start to finish to thwart the evil machinations of saboteurs. Some still maintain to this day that the secrecy that shrouded the development of *ogbunigwe* was the key to success in preventing the enemy from learning how it was built. We sang songs in praise of *ogbunigwe* and some of the guns that Biafran soldiers used. One of the songs in praise of the gun they called Madison went thus:

Imela, Ojukwu imela
Imela, Ojukwu imela
Agam esoro umuaka ibem lay ambush
Were ezigbo Madison gba ndi awusa

meaning:

You have done well Ojukwu, you have done well
You have done well Ojukwu, you have done well
I will join my fellow youngsters and lay ambush
Use a good Madison and shoot Hausa.

I always loved to listen to my uncle's wife, mama Emeka, singing these songs. Some days, while doing her chores, she would spend a better part of the day singing all the Biafran patriotic songs.

In our house, we all learned to pray like my father. His prayers for my brothers always included asking God to guide them so that they would defend our country and come back and meet us all in good condition. One day, during one of our prayer sessions, something dramatic happened: the customary statement that my father used to make in his prayers about the welfare of my brothers was conspicuously absent. Instead of saying God be with Emmanuel and Fidelis, he simply said, "God, as for Fidelis, thy will be done."

That line of prayer was significant to me at the time for the wrong reason. I had always believed that you had to ask God for what you wanted from him, otherwise he would do for you what he desired. I did not particularly like that type of prayer coming from my father. I did not realize that there was a more significant reason why he changed the tune of his prayer. The previous night, my father had a dream which was vivid and trancelike; a voice that seemed real said to him, "Fidelis, your son, has been killed today in the defense of Biafra." He said that when he awoke from the trance, he was overwhelmed with a certain feeling that bordered on dizziness, and then cold sweat started pouring down his body. My father was a deeply religious person who believed very much in biblical miracles. He also believed that if one did the right thing in life, one could always become an instrument through which God spoke. Although he was a social welfare officer who counseled people and tried to restore balance into their lives using a professional and academic approach, he also drew examples from biblical teachings. Because of his spiritual inclinations, he did not see that encounter as an ordinary dream. Instead, he saw it more as a trance in which he had been informed of a true occurrence. When he woke up, he cried for the rest of the night, but tried to contain himself before morning to avoid whipping up alarm in the family. He knew that merely telling my mother that he had a dream that Fidelis had been killed would have had a profound and destructive effect on her. He chose to bear that burden in his mind and never said a word to anyone about it until after the war. He narrated later that when he got up from his bed, he went and washed his face to remove any telltale signs of what had happened to him. The next morning, believing that what he was told in the "trance" was true, he changed his prayer and started asking God to do his will. But even as my father changed his prayer, my mother intensified hers for the protection of my brothers, oblivious of my father's experience.

Most soldiers returned to their homes during the war as often as they could, but that was not Fidelis. He felt, and rightly so, that a soldier's place was on the warfront, not in the rear. The few times he returned home, he always felt irritable anytime he heard the sound of gunfire in Onitsha or environs. As a result, he never really stayed long during those visits and always left hurriedly back to the warfront.

15

Waning Days of the War

As the Biafran war dragged on, out of patriotism people continued to hope that things would soon start going our way. However, there came a time when many began to feel that there was no longer any glimmer of hope for Biafra. Optimism and patriotism started to waver, if not wane completely. Suffering was increasing and starvation was taking a different and more brutal turn. Petty robbery engendered by hunger became rampant; people would actually go to other people's farms and uproot crops that were not even ripe or ready for harvesting and cart them away in sacks for consumption. This included yam, cocoayam and cassava. One day, a thief was apprehended while digging up the yam we planted in our farm; he was caught by some passersby and then handed over to Ezengozi, who brought him to the shade under the mango tree in front of our house. The fair-complexioned but frail-looking man may have been maltreated before he was brought there, because he looked dazed, confused and disheveled all at the same time. His clothes were torn and part of his hair was smeared with mud, and he responded to questions in an awkward and incoherent manner.

We all converged under the mango tree and what seemed like a mini interrogation ensued; gradually, what started with a handfull of people turned into a mini circus. He was asked what his name was and he said, "*Mpotimpo.*" This generated laughter amongst those present, because the name did not sound real. He claimed to be a refugee, implying that he was displaced from another part of Biafra and so had to come to Nnewi to seek sanctuary. His story was unbelievable, because he had a very dense Nnewi accent; it was the general consensus that he was lying about being a refugee. The reason why he was claiming refugee status was because he knew that people would easily forgive a refugee, since they had no farmland in Nnewi to cultivate food for subsistence. They mainly lived in camps and solely depended on relief food coming from CARITAS. If caught stealing, refugees were usually pardoned. It could, however, be said that even though things had gotten very bad in Biafra, it was still believed that a hard-working Nnewi indigene would be able to survive by diligently cultivating his farmland and producing crops, enough to at least feed his family.

As it became even clearer that *Mpotimpo* was an Nnewi indigene, families that had the misfortune of having their crops prematurely harvested by thieves became more infuriated and wanted instant justice. Some people were already gathering whips from an adjacent farmland to commence jungle justice when my father got wind of what was about to take place. He came out and immediately motioned to Ezengozi to release *Mpotimpo*, and Ezengozi obliged without questions. I still believe that this man was maltreated even after he was released because the people around followed him with whips as he slowly walked away instead of running for dear life!

After the war, I started seeing this man around and even discovered that he had a wife and kids. He was actually from my village, and each time I saw him, the name *Mpotimpo* would come to mind. I never for one day held his petty thievery against him because, as my father said when he ordered him released, he was not a real criminal; exigencies of the war and subsequent starvation drove him to do what he had done. I admired that "ruling" from my father on that day, because, even if the man were adjudged guilty, I would not have had the stomach to watch anyone manhandle him under the circumstance. Elsewhere in Nnewi, such petty pilfering continued and the culprits were sometimes caught. Some were seriously dealt with while others were seen as simply trying to survive, especially the refugees.

Trying to survive is an understatement for what was happening then; I do not know of anyone in Nnewi who did not feel the pressure of the war in one way or the other. Some families had lost sons on the warfront, some even lost two people simultaneously. As for my own family, we had not heard from my brothers and anxiety was building. The Biafran currency had almost become worthless. The problem was compounded when Biafra changed her currency and a new one was released. After the change, market women branded the old currency *ngwongwo*, meaning something that was now old and dirty, while they referred to the new currency as *mmege*. I think that the name *mmege* had something to do with being new. Even though Biafrans were instructed to accept both currencies at the same time, until a complete transition was made, some traders still refused to accept *ngwongwo*. Some people unofficially established two separate prices for each commodity; one price (usually higher) when paid for with the old currency, and a different and lower price when paid for with the new currency. The situation became very confused.

In my family, we were feeling the pangs of the war in many ways, but the one that affected me the most, apart from missing my two brothers, was the issue of clothes to wear. My siblings and I had outgrown all the clothes we came back from Lagos with. In my case, all I had left was a pair of trousers that Ijeoma always had to force onto me because they had become so tight that I could not get into them by myself. Anytime we had to go singing with the Voice of Biafran Revolution, Ijeoma would get me ready early so as to have ample time to force the tight trousers gingerly onto me. Whenever I returned from the trip, she would be on hand again to force the trousers off of me. My very good friend, Ubaka Ojukwu, used to tease me about those trousers and called them "tightiny" or "skin trousers." The tightness of the trousers affected my ability to socialize with kids of my age every time we went somewhere with the VOBR to dance to our hallmark music, "L'armor." I was always conscious of the fact that they could come apart at the seams if I stretched them more than necessary. I therefore deliberately avoided certain types of play and kept to myself more often to avoid any provocation that would cause me to start running around. I also had a pair of sandals that I usually wore; I had outgrown them too, but they had ample openings in the front, so when I wore them, about three quarters of my toes would be sticking out in front, beyond the soles. I had to wear them anyway, because I had no other alternative. I am sure that Sam Ojukwu would not have wanted to have a barefooted person in his dance troupe regardless of the circumstance. I knew that I would run out of options in a couple of months when I would have outgrown the shoes and trousers completely. This issue bothered me, and I was already wondering what would happen when I tell Sam Ojukwu that I no longer had clothes nor shoes to go dancing with. I was internally praying for a miracle.

At that juncture, my mother, as usual, pulled off one of the several "miracles" she had become noted for in my life and those of my siblings. Every time one thought that all hope was lost, she would come up with an ingenuous plan that would completely change the dreary outlook and make things better again. That day, some time before noon, she called me up, and with a parcel in her hand, we headed off to the village tailor we called Ekemezie Ilobodo. He was the uncle of my little brother's friend, Chidi Ilobodo. At Ekemezie's house, my mother unwrapped the parcel and handed the contents to the tailor. He smiled wryly, and I realized that the contents of the parcel were a pair of adult trousers and one adult shirt; they both belonged to my father, but he no longer wore them. My mother then gave the tailor some instructions on what she wanted him to do with the clothes and how she wanted him to sew them. Before I knew it, the tailor was taking my measurements; he was whistling with obvious delight that he had work to do.

At that stage during the war, he did not have enough customers to keep him from going hungry. Most people were hungry, and the last thing on their minds at the time was clothing. After my measurements were taken, I went back home with my mother, and just five days later, Ekemezie came to our house with a complete pair of trousers and a shirt. I could not believe that I had a "brand new" set of trousers and shirt to go to "L'armor" with. In my mind, at least I would not be teased by Ubaka anymore. I tried the trousers and they fit, but what struck me was that it was like a patchwork, because there were too many stitches on it. This was because, to make the clothes, Ekemezie had to loosen the stitches on the adult trousers and then, piece by piece, sew them back together to get a fairly continuous piece of cloth from which he then made my own trousers. He succeeded in making it look like a new type of fashion and I feel, to this day, that my friends simply thought that my parents had bought me a pair of new trousers. The shirt was also a piece of patchwork, but it was not as obvious as the trousers. I noticed that the shirt had no collar; of course, collar-less shirts took less material to make. I later found out that the shirt was deliberately sewn that way to save some material. My mother wanted to use material saved from it to add to another piece of cloth she had, and make a shirt for Nnamdi. I was proud of my new patchwork of clothes and never complained. In this day and age, those trousers would be called "jump up," but I did not care—I was happy that my mother had once again performed her miracle. I still had one worry: what would I do when I completely outgrow my sandals? What miracle would my mother perform this time? I thought.

The issue of lack of clothing was rampant; some of the bigger people in our house had to make do with what they could. Ezengozi seemed to wear shorts without shirts all the time. My father collected sacks used to package salt and stockfish by the relief agencies, which were then washed and used by the village tailor to make shorts for the bigger boys. They very much appreciated my father's gesture, but I could not help but notice that every time they came near you, they smelt like stockfish.

Just a few weeks after Ekemezie the tailor brought home my "new clothes", Charles and Obiageli had their own "clothes miracle" in a big way, although they were not in as dire need of clothes as I was. I came back one evening from the spring and Charles excitedly pulled me aside and said that some clothes were sent to them from Britain and that they had just got them. I had initially wanted to argue that it was impossible to bring in something from Britain when I remembered how Ugonna and his sisters traveled out of Biafra, bound for Britain, so I went along with the story. Also, Charles' father was in Britain then, so it was conceivable that he could have sent clothes to them. Much later in the evening, I watched as Charles and Obiageli tried out their new clothes; Charles got a set of pajamas and then two pairs of trousers and shirts to match. Obiageli got about three very beautiful dresses. One of them particularly stands out in my mind to this day; it was yellow or orange in color with a golden chain that doubled as a belt. As a child, of course, I wished that I had someone living overseas to rescue me from the shoe crisis I felt that I was about to experience. From that day on, my cousins always stood out in their new clothes whenever we went out with the VOBR to perform. I was somewhat content with my own "new clothes" because I was no longer teased about how tight my trousers were.

There were many other things we lacked in Biafra; we had no lotions to apply on our bodies after taking baths, and therefore Ijeoma joined in making an improvised lotion from coconut. The nut was ground to shreds using a grate and then coconut oil was squeezed out of the pulp. After further refinement, it was ready to be applied to the body. It gave a glazed and shiny look on the body, a far cry from the dry skin everyone seemed to have developed because of prolonged lack of body lotion. For taking baths we used a homemade soap Aunt Irene made from palm oil and burnt embers of palm fronds. Even though it was homemade, the jet-black-colored soap, called *ncha oka*, always lathered very generously, but I did not particularly like how one smelled after using the soap; it had a characteristic odor that seemed to linger long after use. It was not a particularly pleasant odor but that was our only alternative and one therefore had to make do with it.

The mood in Biafra was generally somber. Through Sam Ojukwu's music, I could tell how well or how badly the war was going. He composed and taught the Voice of Biafran Revolution upbeat songs when things were looking up for Biafra, but taught somber songs when things were not too good. At this time in particular, things were not looking good and he masterfully captured it in a new song he composed. It went thus:

Chineke, nekene umu Biafra.
Kafa n'ebeku gi, biko,
Welu iru amala gi, yikwasi anyi k'uwe
Makana ndi ilo anyi, nacho anyi s'onwu, onwu, onwu, onwu ike

Gini ka umu uwa, ji gba nkiti
Ka Britain, Russia, Egypt, Algeria, na ndi alakuba nine-e
Ndi kwadolu Nigeria fa mebe alu

Ife agha n'eme, agha eliro onye
Onye agbaro oso
Agu guta nke ya, olia ekpokosia

Some of the sayings above are unique to the Igbo dialect but the song generally translates as follows:

Lord, look at your children, Biafrans.
As they cry after you, please
Drape your unending love on us like clothing.
Because our enemies want death for us, catastrophic death!

Why did people of the world keep silent?
As Britain, Russia, Egypt, Algeria and other Muslim nations
People who are supporting Nigeria to commit atrocities

This is what war brings, if you do not die
If you are not displaced
Hunger will bring its own scourge and sickness will compound matters.

The part of the song that talked about hunger was very timely because at that time there were many people afflicted with *kwashiorkor* all over Biafra, especially children, and hundreds were dying daily.

As I write this part of the book on my computer at exactly 7:25 a.m. on Sunday morning, February 10, 2002, I can feel a nostalgic but sad memory of what happened in those years, especially at the time I was describing. People were dying of different things, some from hunger and *kwashiorkor*, some from air raids that the federal side was visiting on Biafran civilians and many were obviously dying on the warfront. Many women were burying their sons, who were casualties in the war, while others were burying their young ones who died of *kwashiorkor* or other treatable diseases that we could not treat because of a lack of medication. Diseases like malaria became very deadly; ordinary wounds easily killed people because tetanus injections were not available. It is therefore usually a surprise to me when I hear people character-ize the Biafran experience as simply a war in which about two million people died. There was more to it, and when the emotional upset that this harrowing experience brought to bear on the masses is factored into the general scheme of things, it becomes obvious that the war took a far heavier toll on Biafrans than had originally been estimated or ever thought possible. There were peo-ple who could not bear what they were witnessing and so went insane; there were those who could not deal with the human losses their families sustained so they died of broken hearts—the list of the after effects of the war is endless.

It was now 1969, I believe, and the federal troops were permanently sta-tioned in Onitsha, which is a couple of miles away from Nnewi; day in day out, you would hear the sounds of war machines punctuated by the deafening sounds of heavy artillery. There was no respite for the people living around the Onitsha area. Every time things heated up and the sound of gunfire per-meated the air, I would always withdraw to one corner and wonder about my brothers in the battlefield; I would silently ask God to be with them. As much as I wanted to remain optimistic about the Biafran war and its final outcome, I could no longer see reason to; Biafra was truly under siege and there was no escape route. I felt that it would only be a matter of time before the federal troops closed in to finish the havoc they started earlier in the North in 1966.

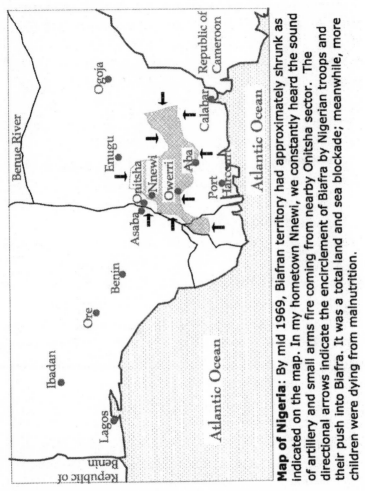

Map of Nigeria: By mid 1969, Biafran territory had approximately shrunk as indicated on the map. In my hometown Nnewi, we constantly heard the sound of artillery and small arms fire coming from nearby Onitsha sector. The directional arrows indicate the encirclement of Biafra by Nigerian troops and their push into Biafra. It was a total land and sea blockade; meanwhile, more children were dying from malnutrition.

The other thing that exacerbated this terrible feeling of mine was the story we were hearing about the activities of saboteurs in Biafra. They were said to be transmitting tactical information about the movement of Biafran troops to the enemy, and so every step Biafran troops tried to make was actually check-mated by the federal troops because they had inside information. This was killing me. I recalled that the unceremonious withdrawal of Biafran soldiers from the town of Ore, a few miles from Lagos, in

September of 1967, was attributed to the activities of saboteurs. It was said that Biafran commanders in charge of that operation sabotaged it by halting the forward advancement of the soldiers. As this was happening, Nigerian troops had the time to regroup and push Biafran soldiers back into the Midwest. It was a large-scale disaster and the story dampened the upbeat spirits of many in Biafra. I remembered that after the failure of that operation in 1967, three Biafran commanders, Col. Victor Banjo, Major Philip Alale and Lt. Col. Emmanuel Ifeajuna, were tried by a military tribunal, found guilty of sabotaging the operation and executed by firing squad. It was said that Lt. Col. Ifeajuna was the ringleader. That was the first time I personally ever heard the word *Sabo*, which was the short form for saboteur. According to the story, when Col. Ifeajuna was about to be executed, he was asked if he had any parting statement and he purportedly said, "My plans are intact, even after I am executed, the plans I put in place will be actualized." For the record, there was never an official verification of the statement credited to Ifeajuna, but many in Biafra suggested that the reason why Ifeajuna purportedly sabotaged the mission was because he and the other commanders were paid by the federal troops. There was a song that we used to sing in Biafra in response to the Ifeajuna debacle. It went thus:

Unu afugo, Ife nzuzu wetalu n'uwa?
Akpili ego, Ifeajuna lel'anyi

Unu afugo, nwanne na nwanne jel' agha?
Nwanne puo n'uzo, le nwanne ya

meaning:

Have you ever seen what stupidity brought to the world?
Money hungry Ifeajuna sold us
Have you ever seen? Siblings went to war
One sibling went and sold the other

After the war, when I was in the secondary school, my class two Geography teacher, Mr. Mmaduakor, told us that he went to school at the Dennis Memorial Grammar School, Onitsha, with Emmanuel Ifeajuna. He referred to Ifeajuna as sharp but exceedingly rascally and I always wondered if being rascally had anything to do with the duplicitous behavior ascribed to him? Mr. Mmaduakor also said that Ifeajuna represented Nigeria in the Olympics, prior to the war, as a high jumper. All these caused me to wonder why someone who had everything going for him threw it all away by betraying Biafra.

Anyway, since the Ifeajuna episode took place at the very start of the war, people like me thought that *sabo* activity was over and done with, but at this stage in 1969, from what we were hearing, it seemed as though *sabo* activity was actually intensifying, and Biafra was feeling the effect.

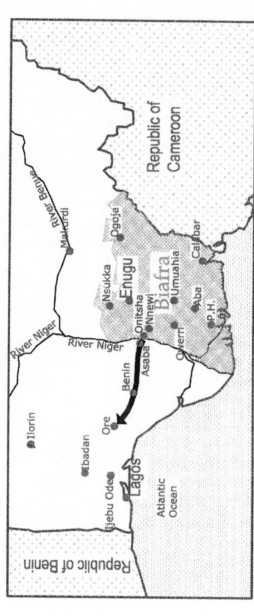

Map of Nigeria. The arrow indicates the approximate path of Biafran soldiers who crossed the River Niger at Onitsha, in August 1967, took control of the midwest and marched as far as Ore. We were all estatic when news of the incursion came but later, morale nose-dived in Biafra as the troops were said to have retreated back into the midwest in Sept. 1967 and later beaten back into Onitsha.

Col. Victor Banjo, the Biafran officer incharge of the incursion, was later executed along with Lt. Col. Ifeajuna, Major Philip Alale and Samuel Agbam. They were said to be saboteurs for their actions in the retreat of Biafra from Ore.

In the midst of the *sabo* problem, something devastating occurred! My father had just returned from work one afternoon and was listening to the radio—he may have been listening to Radio Yaounde, Cameroon. Cameroon is the African country next to Nigeria, to the east. My father usually tuned into their radio station hoping to get unbiased information about the progress of the war. He was listening to the radio when he suddenly belched out the words "Elohim Israel!" Everyone around turned towards him and for a moment he said nothing. At first, he just looked nervous and then his eyes started glistening as though he was about to shed tears. I did not want to witness the episode of my father crying, so I momentarily looked away. My mother must have said, "*Nna Fide ogini*" (Fide's father, what is wrong?) many times before he collected himself, cleared his throat and in an unsteady voice said, "The great Zik has left Biafra!" I knew that Zik was Nigeria's one-time leader, but I did not immediately grasp the significance of his departure from Biafra, and when my father said this, I was not even sure where Zik went. As my father composed himself a little, he sought to clarify what he had earlier said, so he restated that the radio had just announced that Zik had left Biafra. Apparently, Dr. Nnamdi "Zik" Azikiwe, an Igbo who became the very first President of Nigeria immediately after her Independence in 1960, had defected to Nigeria.

Dr. Azikiwe's defection caused quite a stir in Biafra and demoralized many. As an international figure before the Biafran war started, it was thought that his stay in Biafra lent credence to the Biafran cause; some felt he could work as an emissary for Biafra, going overseas and convincing Harold Wilson and his cabinet that Biafra was actually being oppressed. The story of Zik's defection caught many Biafrans by surprise. There was an argument where some people surmised that he may have been unhappy with Ojukwu all this time and may simply have waited for the right time to make his move. They argued that even though Zik had now abandoned Biafra, we might have lost nothing, because when he was in Biafra, he did practically nothing to help the Biafran cause. They insisted that a man of

Zik's stature should have been able to do more in the international circles by getting many countries to recognize Biafra. I felt terrible about the turn of events, because the more I understood the importance of Zik with respect to the Biafran cause, the more I wondered why he chose that line of action. I wondered if he was unaware of the plight of Biafrans, the people dying daily in the warfront, the children dying of starvation and the scourge that was *kwashiorkor*. I wondered how heartless one could be to have done what he did.

The defection became even more painful when I recalled that Zik was said to have written the first version of Biafra's national anthem, titled "Be Still My Soul." For the record, when I visited the United States in 1979, I heard the instrumental version of the Biafran national anthem on the radio and at first I thought that someone in the radio station had played it by accident. When the song ended, the announcer mentioned one Jean Sibelius as the composer. I conducted further research on this issue and discovered that the name of the song was "Finlandia Hymn." The original words of the hymn by the Finnish composer, Jean Sibelius, were incidentally protesting against the Russian oppression of Finland in the early part of the 20th century. I do not know how Biafra ended up using an existing song as her national anthem when we had outstanding musicologists like Sam Ojukwu who would have developed a unique national anthem for Biafra in a heartbeat. Having said that, though, I still find myself agog with emotion every time I hear that song; its lack of originality has not in any way taken away from the emotion it evokes in me.

The thought about Zik's defection never left my mind because in 1979, when Nigeria became a democracy again, he came to Nnewi to campaign for Nigeria's presidency under the umbrella of Nigerian People's Party. As I listened to him at the Nkwo Nnewi field, near the roundabout, I could not help but wonder if I should believe what he was saying or if I should actually take it with a grain of salt. In my mind, I felt that when the going would get tough again, the great Zik might jump ship. I was not alone in that thought because this issue later became a nagging campaign question which he had to field at every campaign stop. He explained his defection as a well-orchestrated strategy to help end the war and stop the suffering of the masses. Whatever the reason was, I believe that posterity will judge what happened as people shed their cloaks of fear and begin to honestly tell the story of what they really saw, heard and felt. I must state that from my point of view, that singular action that Zik took precluded him from getting the votes of many Igbo people during the 1979 elections. One of the curious questions I have always had was, How was Zik spirited out of Biafra into the federal side without detection? I would still like to know how that feat was accomplished.

Whatever the case may be, it must be said that Zik's absence was felt in the whole of Biafra; some saw it as sign of surrender, others felt he was just ahead of his time and knew that there was no hope for Biafra. Some simply felt that he had betrayed Biafra.

As we were still groping for reasons to believe that the Biafran cause could be sustained, even in the face of biting enemy siege, something that seemed to offer some hope occurred—we heard that Biafran commandos were about to mount an unbelievable assault on the federal troops in Onitsha. As if to buttress what we heard, one day a convoy of commandos passed through Nnewi; they were headed for Onitsha sector for the proposed assault and we were all ecstatic. I cannot tell how many soldiers passed through, but from the perspective of a little boy, I deign to guess that they must have numbered several thousands, all clad in commando assault outfits with all manner of guns. The kids dutifully stood in line, in front of the compound of Mr. Albert Igbokwe, admiring them in their "camo" as they filed by. They were coming from Oraifite and going to Nkwo Nnewi, from where they would proceed to Onitsha for the assault. We were devastated when we later heard that the planned assault did not go well because they had once again been sabotaged! That was painful; yet, in thinking about the final version of the Biafran national anthem which says "…we must defend our lives or we shall perish…," it was imperative that the Biafrans continued to try, even in the face of mounting setbacks.

Many details of the war are still so fresh in my mind that sometimes I wonder if I am ever going to be able to put the whole episode behind me. As I write, I feel like I am witnessing events all over again. For example, I can still remember all the words of the first stanza of the Biafran national anthem as though I just memorized them yesterday. Yet I recall that I learned the song about 34 years ago! These are the full words of the Biafran national anthem.

Land of the rising sun, we love and cherish,
Beloved homeland of our brave heroes;
We must defend our lives or we shall perish,
We shall protect our hearts from all our foes;
But if the price is death for all we hold dear,
Then let us die without a shred of fear.

Hail to Biafra, consecrated nation,
Oh fatherland, this be our solemn pledge:
Defending thee shall be a dedication,
Spilling our blood we'll count a privilege;
The waving standard which emboldens the free
Shall always be our flag of liberty.

We shall emerge triumphant from this ordeal,
And through the crucible unscathed we'll pass;
When we are poised the wounds of battle to heal,
We shall remember those who died in mass;
Then shall our trumpets peal the glorious song
Of victory we scored o'er might and wrong.

Oh God, protect us from the hidden pitfall,
Guide all our movements lest we go astray;
Give us the strength to heed the humanist call:

'To give and not to count the cost" each day;
Bless those who rule to serve with resoluteness,
To make this clime a land of righteousness.

16

The War Ends

From 1969 onwards, things never really got better in Biafra; they continued to wax from bad to worse. Conscription was on the rise and young men seemed to always do what was necessary to avoid going to the war. We continued to take things one day at a time and the year 1969 passed, ushering in a new year, 1970. Immediately, the Voice of Biafran Revolution learned an English song, which went thus:

Faith of Biafra
Living strong
In spite of fire
OAU, silent
British, Egyptians and Russians and all...

Even though the song talked about Biafra's faith living strong, it was to me more of a cry for help to the whole world and the Organization of African Unity, so that they would not stand on the sidelines and watch as Biafra was being methodically decapitated. Everywhere one looked, tragedy would be staring one in the face. Children with *kwashiorkor* had increased in number even though some had been airlifted to the countries that recognized Biafra not too long before. *Kwashiorkor* seemed to have assumed a different but brutal turn. The kids now looked like "walking skeletons" and one could easily count their ribs even from a distance; their eyeballs sunk deeper into their cavities and shone as white as snow. There seemed to be no hope.

During the very first days of January 1970, the army conscriptors came again to our village, and as usual young men started scattering in all directions. The soldiers went to a neighboring compound and one of the young men was about to scale a wall and run away when out of frustration, one of the soldiers shot him on the leg and he instantly became incapacitated. Of course, he was no longer fit to serve in the army and many people were alarmed that the conscription effort had gone to that extreme.

Then came January 12. The day started like other days before it; the morning sun seemed to have risen early and Mamaocha, as usual, had gone to Nkwo Nnewi market. My father had gone to work while my mother attended to her patients in her maternity home. In the compound, we were playing the game of *ncholokoto*. All of a sudden, some of the women who had gone to the market in the morning started returning to the villages in groups. It was very unusual because they stayed in the market till sometime after 4:30 p.m. every day. There was also something unusual about the way that the women were excitedly chattering amongst themselves as they made their ways into the village and their compounds. It did not take long for us to find out what they were excitedly discussing; they said that Nigerian soldiers just drove into Nkwo Nnewi market in land rovers and were driving up and down the road. The story continued that if you said "one Nigeria" to them, they would give you beans, rice and cigarettes. There was disbelief; some women immediately took off for the market to see things for themselves. The men did not even attempt to go out because they felt that it might be a ploy by the federal troops. That was exactly how the Asaba massacre started during the initial stages of the war; villagers were lured out and killed in large numbers. This time, people wanted to be cautious in case the soldiers had come back to finish what they had started in Asaba earlier on. Everywhere was quiet; there was no jubilation; people moved about within the villages and in low tones, talked about what was happening. Later, people who had gone to see things for themselves came back, some with foodstuff, proving that the whole thing was not a ruse.

I was now a 10-year-old boy who had been forced by circumstances engendered by the war to mature ahead of my age mentally, but I did not know how to view what was unfolding. As much as I wanted the suffering to end, I knew that the entry of the Federal troops into Nnewi, which was probably the last line of defense for Biafra, meant that Biafra had been defeated. I broke down and cried. All the songs we sang about Biafra and her ability to withstand Nigeria's aggression came back to me. I remembered all the prayers we offered to God and the hope we had that since Biafra's foundation was rooted in the belief that God was with us, we would prevail. I was disappointed and devastated. My concern then shifted to my brothers. I thought to myself that the troops must have overrun Biafran soldiers and probably wiped them out before getting to Nnewi. I thought of the Biafran soldiers of the Eleventh Division stationed in Nnewi and wondered why we did not hear any exchange of gunfire between them and the Nigerian troops. Did they give up without a fight? Were they surprised and overrun? I wondered. All these concerns were swirling through my head but I could not do much but wait like every other person to see what happened next.

Ezengozi then did something that made me feel really sad. He drew the picture of a hand with the index finger raised and then put an inscription on it which read, "One Nigeria." I was not amused, but I did not immediately tell him. I wondered why so many people had already started singing the praises of the federal troops. I wondered why Ezengozi made the sudden change from "Long Live Biafra" to "One Nigeria." I felt that it was too soon to abandon Biafra and start praising the same soldiers who had been decimating our population for the past three years. No one knew exactly what the situation was, even though many had gone to the market and actually saw the soldiers. It later became clear that the reason why Ezengozi made the drawing was because of the anticipation that federal soldiers would be going from house to house to seek out those who still questioned their "victory." In case that happened, he wanted to have something handy to point to as evidence that he had accepted. The Asaba massacre, in which he lost his father, uncle, brother and other relatives, was still fresh in his mind; he knew how ruthless the soldiers could be and did not want to take any chances.

This was how events unfolded in those days. Apparently, General Chukwuemeka Odumegwu Ojukwu left Biafra along with some of his advisers on the 10th of January. On the 11th, a message which he had pre-recorded was broadcast to the nation. [*full text in appendix*] In that message, he told Biafrans that he had gone in search of peace and had handed over the leadership of Biafra to one of her commanders, Major General Phillip Effiong. After General Ojukwu's departure, Biafra's new leader embarked on an intense negotiation with the Nigerian government. When negotiations were completed on the 12th of January, he made a broadcast to the nation on the true situation of things. Below is the full text of that speech (*courtesy, Dawodu.com*)

Fellow Countrymen,

As you know, I was asked to be the officer administering the government of this republic on the 10th of January 1970. Since then, I know that some of you have been waiting to hear a statement from me. I have had extensive consultations with the leaders of the community, both military and civil, and I am now encouraged and hasten to make this statement to you by the mandate of the Armed Forces and the people of this country. I have assumed the leadership of the government.

Throughout history, injured people have had to resort to arms in their self-defense where peaceful negotiations fail. We are no exception. We took up arms because of the sense of insecurity generated in our people by the events of 1966. We have fought in defense of that cause.

I take this opportunity to congratulate officers and men of our Armed Forces for their gallantry and bravery, which have earned for them the admiration of the whole world. I thank the civil population for their steadfastness and courage in the face of overwhelming odds and starvation. I am convinced that the suffering of our people must be brought to an immediate end. Our people are now disillusioned, and those elements of the old government regime who have made negotiations and reconciliation impossible have voluntarily removed themselves from our midst.

I have, therefore, instructed an orderly disengagement of troops. I am dispatching emissaries to make contact with Nigeria's field commanders in places like Onitsha, Owerri, Awka, Enugu, and Calabar with a view to arranging armistice. I urge on General Gowon, in the name of humanity, to order his troops to pause while an armistice is negotiated in order to avoid the mass suffering caused by the movement of population.

We have always believed that our differences with Nigeria should be settled by peaceful negotiations. A delegation of our people is therefore ready to meet representatives of Nigeria Federal Government anywhere to negotiate a peace settlement on the basis of OAU resolutions. The delegation will consist of the Chief Justice Sir Louis Mbanefo, as leader, Professor Eni Njoku, Mr. J. I. Emembolu, Chief A.E. Bassey, Mr. E. Agumah. The delegation will have full authority to negotiate on our behalf. I have appointed a council to advise me on the government of the country. It consists of the Chief Justice Sir Louis Mbanefo, Brigadier P.C. Amadi—Army, Brigadier C. A. Nwawo—Army, Captain W. A. Anuku—Navy, Wing Commander J. I. Ezero—Air Force, Inspector-General of Police, Chief P. I. Okeke, Attorney-General Mr. J. I. Emembolu, Professor Eni Njoku, Dr. I. Eke, Chief A.E. Udofia, Chief A.E. Bassey, Mr. M.T. Mbu, Mr. E. Agumah, Chief Frank Opuigo, Chief J.N. Echeruo. Any question of a government in exile is repudiated by our people.

Civilian population are hereby advised to remain calm and to cooperate with the Armed Forces and the Police in the maintenance of law and order. They should remain in their homes and stop mass movements, which have increased suffering and loss of lives.

On behalf of our people, I thank those foreign governments and friends who have steadfastly given us support in our cause. We shall continue to count on their continued help and counsel. I also thank His Holiness the Pope, the Joint Church Aid and other relief organizations for the help they have given for the relief of suffering and starvation. I appeal to all governments to give urgent help for relief and to prevail on the Federal Military Government to order their troops to stop all military operations.

May God help us all.

I respect General Effiong because of his courage. To many he is a hero. It took courage to accept the leadership of a nation that had practically been wiped out; it took courage to step in and commence negotiations, knowing that his own life was in danger, too. It took enormous courage to say what he said in that speech. He did not attempt to make patronizing remarks about Nigeria just because Biafra had become a defeated people. He made all the necessary points that needed to be made in that speech, including putting on record the fact that Biafra fought because we were an injured people and that it was customary for injured people to pick up arms to defend themselves. For this, I salute this man of courage and hope that he will go down in history as one of the true heroes of Biafra.

Meanwhile, some Biafran soldiers on the warfront had become aware of the fact that the war had ended, so they started returning to the villages. Some told stories of their encounter with the federal troops as they made their journey home; the Nigerian soldiers were said to have shot Biafran soldiers who were still wearing their uniforms or failed to pay "proper homage" to them as the "victors." For fear of what the federal troops might do to them, some Biafran soldiers did not truly identify themselves. Many quickly burnt their army uniforms and did away with their rifles. There were some die-hards amongst them who refused to give up or dispose of their guns; they hid them and anticipated that should the federal troops attempt to assault the villages, they would pick up their arms and respond in kind.

Ironically, all this was happening just a few days after Biafran soldiers had shot a young man in my village, on the leg, for attempting to evade conscription. It was always a subject of discussion that this tragic incident happened just two days before the end of the war. I do not recall what became of the man.

After General Effiong's statement, General Gowon responded at midnight on the same day. Below is the full text of his own speech (*courtesy, Dawodu.com*):

My Dear Compatriots:

We have arrived at one of the greatest moments of the history in our nation. A great moment of victory for national unity and reconciliation. We have arrived at the end of a tragic and painful conflict.

Thirty months ago we were obliged to take up arms against our brothers, who were deceived and misled into armed rebellion against their fatherland by the former Lieut-Col. Ojukwu. Our objective was to crush the rebellion; to maintain the territorial integrity of our nation; to assert the ability of the black man to build a strong, progressive and prosperous modern state and to ensure respect, dignity and equality in the comity of nations for our posterity.

I salute you once again for the courage, loyalty and steadfastness of our fighting troops, and the loyal support and sacrifice of all Nigerians. I pay tribute to the courage and resourcefulness of those who have fought so long against lawful troops, as victims of Ojukwu's vicious propaganda and the machinations of certain foreign governments.

You will have heard the broadcast of Lieut.-Col. Effiong asking the remnants of the secessionist troops to lay down their arms. This is in accord with our appeal. I accept in good faith Lieut.-Colonel Effiong's declaration accepting the OAU resolutions supporting the unity and territorial integrity of Nigeria. I urge all the secessionist troops to act honorably and lay down their arms in an orderly manner. Instructions have been issued to all field commanders of their Nigerian Army to put into immediate effect to contingency arrangements for the mass surrender of secessionist forces. The officers of the secessionist troops are urged to send emissaries to federal field commanders at once to work out detailed arrangements for orderly surrender. All field commanders will take all necessary measures to give full protection to surrendering troops. Field commanders are instructed to push and establish effective federal presence in all areas remaining under secessionist control. Federal troops in carrying out this directive will be accompanied by police units and will exercise all care and shoot only if they encounter resistance. I appeal to all remaining secessionist forces to co-operate with federal troops to avoid any further loss of life. All federal troops must continue to observe the letter and spirit of the code of conduct issued at the beginning of the military operations.

We reiterate our promise of a general amnesty for all those misled into the futile attempt to disintegrate the country. Federal troops, East-Central State officials and authorized relief workers in the field will take adequate care of all civilians in the liberated areas. We must all demonstrate our will for honourable reconciliation within a united Nigeria.

Fellow countrymen, with your continued loyalty and dedication to the national cause, we shall succeed in healing the nation's wounds. We must all welcome, with open arms, the people now freed from the tyranny and deceit of Ojukwu and his gang.

Long live one united Nigeria.

We thank God for His mercies.

Even though the statement from Gowon indicated that there would be no reprisals against Biafrans, most men in Biafra expected some form of it and never really felt free to move around. Then came the rumor that the federal soldiers were going around the villages, harassing and beating people who had any type of guns in their homes, even double-barrel guns. As a result, families that had double-barrel guns started scrambling to hide or dispose of them. It was also rumored that the mere mention of the name Biafra brought the wrath of the federal troops on Biafrans.

Once it became clear that the war had ended, my aunt, Mrs. Edozien and her family started getting ready to go back to Asaba. Ezengozi was also going to go along. That was a very painful moment for Nnamdi and me. We had practically become so close to Charles and Obiageli that separation was difficult to imagine. Regardless of how we felt, their departure was set and I was completely devastated. The day before they left, they all started packing their belongings as I sorrowfully watched; all the good times we had together started coming back to me; I remembered the Boy Scout trips with Charles and the fun we all had together; I remembered the VOBR and our dancing outings; I remembered the war games we played; I also remembered how Charles silenced the refugee boy, Ejima, by beating him up and how he no longer waylaid and pelted stones at us whenever we went to *Anaoji* to play. I just could not believe that it was ending so soon.

On the day of their departure, we all woke up early, got ready and practically the whole of my family accompanied them to the nkwo Nnewi Motor Park, carrying their belongings. I do not remember what happened to my aunt's car, but I know that it was not in our convoy. We slowly walked down the dusty road and the elders talked about the end of the war and what had been happening since then, while Charles and I silently followed. At the motor park, they boarded a vehicle, we all bid them goodbye and Ezengozi muttered something like, "We will see you soon." I could not stand it and immediately broke down and started crying while we walked back the way we came. Back home, Nnamdi and I started adjusting to the absence of our cousins.

After the war, regardless of the fact that people felt that the education we had during the war amounted to very little in substance and value, I stepped up to elementary 4 at the St. Mary's School. East Central State was the new name of Biafra as imposed on it by General Gowon. He appointed Anthony Ukpabi Asika administrator for the East Central State; the man hailed from Onitsha, but he was on the federal side during the war and supported Nigeria. Many felt that General Gowon was simply rewarding him for his allegiance to Nigeria. It was also rumored that Gowon did not trust any Igbo to lead the East Central State, hence his appointment of a man who was anti-Igbo during the war. Igbos despised Ukpabi Asika; he was given all kinds of derogatory nicknames, all pointing to the fact that he was a sellout. He had an annoying goatee and always wore a smile that smacked of sadism.

As some families quickly started making plans to go back to where they lived before the war, my father had resolved to stay permanently in the East Central State. He felt betrayed by what his Hausa friend, *Sajin Major*, wanted to do to him in Lagos before the war started. He was bent on preventing that type of scenario from ever occurring again, so he chose to stay in the town of Aguata, where he was the social welfare officer. Initially, he shuttled from Nnewi to Aguata and back on a daily basis. My mother also resolved to stay in Nnewi, where her maternity clinic had taken hold and was doing well. We, the kids, actually wished we could go back to Lagos to resume a life that was interrupted by the civil war and probably have the chance to once again see our old friends, but that did not happen. Our dreams were dashed and we learned to accept the idea of living in the village. Even though we were not born in the village, many years' stay in Nnewi had turned us into village people. We could speak Nnewi dialect as well as those born there; we could go to the bush and fetch firewood like others; we could go to Okpuani, the village spring, to fetch water, and heck,

I could make some of the crafts that those born in the village were noted for. The transformation was complete and we were completely assimilated.

In spite of the fact that the war had ended, I was still very bitter and my anger was directed at the federal side. My brother Fidelis was still missing and we did not know whether he was alive. Emmanuel was also missing. The last we heard was that the Federal troops had cut off Emmanuel's battalion in Ohafia. Essentially, my two brothers who went to the Biafran war to defend her territorial integrity, were not back and there was no sign of where they were. My mother was undeterred; her faith in God and belief that all would be well was unshaken. Every week, she would gather all the kids, invite some of our friends and offer what she called *salaka*. She would make food and several other goodies. The children would take turns and pray to God to save Fidelis and Emmanuel and bring them back safely. We would then sing several songs, such as "Oh Lord, deliver Fidelis and Emmanuel, Oh Lord deliver them, oh Lord deliver them…" The kids loved it because of the food and other goodies my mother served, but it was painful for Nnamdi and I because we had become aware of the gravity of what was happening; our big brothers had vanished in the war! The implication was very frightening to imagine.

A disturbing trend quickly began to emerge; some people in Nnewi capitalized on the absence of my brothers and began to prey on my poor mother! As soon as they found out that my brothers had not returned from the war, rumors about their supposed sightings became rife and my mother was subjected to an unbelievable emotional roller coaster! Any time someone told her about sightings of any of my brothers, she would give the person some money in appreciation and then ask for more details. Usually after a while, the trail would grow cold. She never relented; many so-called prophets became our friends because my mother always had our doors open to them. They would come, pray, give their visions (which to me were always ambiguous), get some money and leave. The types of visions they gave were the ambiguous types that could be interpreted many ways; we had no choice than to follow along.

I never knew where my father stood in all this, but I do know that he always looked irritable. He developed heart palpitations, but never told anyone that he was having sleepless nights because of the absence of his sons. In the mornings, he would still wake up and go to work not telling anyone what he was feeling. My mother, on the other hand, poured out her heart at the slightest opportunity. I believe it helped her manage the pain.

One sunny Monday morning, I was at my mother's maternity home, which was located in the compound of Mr. Nweze Obiazi, bless him. This man gave my mother one of the buildings in his compound, free of charge, to set up the Uzoma Maternity Home during the war. He did not ask for a penny in return; the satisfaction he had was that Biafran children were being helped to avoid *kwashiorkor* and that pregnant women were helped through the prenatal and antenatal stages, and in the actual delivery of their babies. In turn, my mother treated, free of charge, women who could not afford their medical bills. At the end of the war, Mr. Obiazi insisted that my mother should continue to use his building until she built a new and modern maternity home.

At the maternity, Mondays were always busy for my mother; she delivered lectures to pregnant women about good nutrition and then followed them with pre—and postnatal consultations. She always had a full house because, at that time, Uzoma Maternity was the major maternity in Nnewi and the surrounding area. Women came to deliver babies from as far away neighboring villages and towns as Otolo, Nnewichi, Ojoto, Ichi, Uruagu, Umudim, Osumenyi, Ukpor, Ozubulu, Oraifite, Oba, Awka Etiti and Nnobi. The crowd of pregnant women in the compound every Monday was always unbelievable. Market women saw the gathering as opportunity to come and sell food to the pregnant women, resulting in the fact that on some Mondays, someone who did not know any better, could mistake the grounds of the maternity for a market place

That day, I had come to the maternity compound to buy *elele* and *akara*. Both are delicacies made from black-eyed peas or beans. I had already purchased what I wanted and was getting ready to leave when I saw a tall, unkempt man or boy approaching the maternity. The compound had a low wall around it, which acted as a security fence, but one could easily see above it. I wondered what this mentally deranged man was coming to the maternity to do. His hair was not cut and had a dirty, Rastafarian look. For a moment, my attention was drawn away from the man as my mother came out of her consulting room. By the time I looked again, the man had walked into the maternity compound. I cannot capture in words what transpired in that moment, for right at that instance, my mother let out a shrill shout of "*nekwanu Emma.*" She must have jumped over the two or three steps that led outside from where she was; she ran up to the man and embraced him and they both fell on the dusty ground. I was still glued to where I was standing until they fell, and as if someone gave the crowd of women a go ahead order to react, they spontaneously ran towards them and started embracing their now dusty bodies. I was speechless and out of joy, I ran as fast as I could back home to alert everyone that Emmanuel was back. He was immediately given some food, which he hurriedly ate and then fainted. He later came to and they all came back home. My father was not at home when Emmanuel returned and I have no memory of what he did when he first saw him but I know that he was overjoyed. Our emotional burden was cut in half instantly. Visitors were coming and going and offering their congratulatory messages while others simply gave thanks to God for his mercies. While we celebrated Emma's return, Fidelis' absence was still bothering everyone, but my mother seemed buoyed up and hoped that the same type of miracle that happened in Emmanuel's case would apply to Fidelis.

Emmanuel later recalled the events leading up to his return. After his troop was cut off at Uzoakoli by the federal troops, they embarked on Operation Open Corridor, fighting their way out of the blockade and taking an untold number of casualties. Many Biafran women who had come to buy food from behind enemy lines perished in that conflict. Some had infants who were either abandoned on the warfront when things got very bad or who were killed. I recall a story he narrated. The federal troops were enveloping their location and they were trying very hard to avoid detection by crawling on their stomachs. Meanwhile, bullets were whizzing by, coming from snipers stationed all around them. Just as their commander called for absolute silence from all, an infant that one of the women on *afia attack* was carrying suddenly started crying. The lady was warned to get the infant to stop crying. The more she tried, the more the baby cried. That noise seemed to intensify the gunfire directed at their location so one of the soldiers got hold of the baby and crushed it. Instant silence ensued.

Emmanuel narrated that once it became clear that the war had ended, it was every man for himself. He took off his army uniform on the advice of the villagers, who insisted that the federal troops were still embarking on reprisal killings of Igbo soldiers. From there, he started his journey home on foot, as no one would give him a ride because he looked like a mad boy with his hair unkempt. For food, he ate palm kernel nuts and then drank anything that was flowing, in the name of water. The only ride he got was at Ozubulu, near Nnewi, after he had helped a taxi driver push his vehicle; the driver allowed him in for a little while and then asked him to step down. He then journeyed the rest of the way back to Nnewi, to my mother's maternity home.

One evening we were all sitting behind my grandmother's kitchen. Ijeoma was cooking dinner and Emmanuel was talking to her, trying to catch up with what he missed while he was gone. Emmanuel is six years older than I am, so I was too young to partake in their conversation, yet I was listening attentively. A conversation came up about Fidelis and Emmanuel said that he had heard that Fidelis was killed in the war. I was devastated and confused, and the only reaction I had was to walk away instantly. I went to our room and cried; I recall that I was so emotionally upset that my body shook violently. As I cried, I was working very hard not to alert anyone, because I was not sure what to say was the reason why I was crying. After a while, the thought of my mother came to me; I wondered what she would do if indeed Fidelis had been killed. Emmanuel's return had buoyed up her belief that her prayers were working, and for all she knew we were going to continue to offer *salaka* to God and the miracle in Emmanuel's case would be repeated. I had no reason to think that Emmanuel did not know what he was saying, after all, he just came back from the warfront and was in a much better position to tell. Much later, I quietly went to Ijeoma and said, "Did you hear what Emmanuel said about Fidelis?" She just said, "I do not believe it," and then quickly walked away. I was not sure what to make of her reaction, but from then on, I began to waver internally about my strongly held belief that Fidelis may still be alive. I did not want my mother to sense my resignation, so I diligently attended the *salakas* she organized, where other kids were invited and we prayed for Fidelis' safe return and had refreshments. As days turned into weeks and weeks into months, Fidelis' absence was becoming unnerving. The number of soldiers still returning had become reduced to a trickle.

I always feel a sense of pride in Emmanuel every time I remember that he went to the war at age fifteen. Also, whenever I remember the circumstances under which he went to that war, I respect him even more. As recently as in the year 2001, I sent him an email to thank him, because I felt that I never really formally did thank him for rising up to the challenge. My hope is that Igbos would continue to cherish the sacrifice made by Emmanuel, Fidelis and other Biafran soldiers. They defended Biafra to the very end and some laid down their lives in the process. Emmanuel was put on the spot but he did not shirk the responsibility. He is a true Biafran hero.

Elsewhere in Nnewi, people were beginning to pick up the pieces of their lives. Families that lost loved ones were now having formal funeral rites for them, and that became the order of the day. In Nnewi, funeral ceremonies included displays of masquerades like *Ikedinodogwu*, *Ozokwamkpo, ayakuzikwonsi* and more. The kids always went to these funeral ceremonies to watch the masquerades perform; most young men, who just came back from the army and did not yet have substantive things to do, joined the masquerade troupes. Emmanuel quickly joined *Ozokwamkpo ndi Okpunoeze*, a masquerade troupe organized by my clan.

During this period, many church leaders started decrying the fact that young Christian men were joining the masquerade groups in droves. They cautioned that it was a form of paganism and that Christians should refrain from participating in such acts. In fact there was a tacit threat that all Christians who joined the masquerade groups might be excommunicated from the churches. To counter the assertions of the church leaders, a slogan, which was coined by the leaders of the masquerade troupes, quickly emerged. It went thus: "*Ozokwamkpo anaro uka, uka di n'obi ,*" which means that being a member of the masquerade club does not stop one from going to church. This argument continued, and later, some Christian families gradually started pulling their loved ones out of the masquerade groups. Emmanuel left *Ozokwamkpo Okpunoeze.*

My father was still shuttling from home to Aguata, where he worked. It was a distance of about twenty miles and he used his car, which had served him well throughout the war. He usually left the house every morning at about 6:30 a.m. and returned around 5:00 p.m. The road from Nnewi to Aguata was bad and dusty; every time he came back from work, he looked like he had spent a better part of the day outside. Of course, the car had no air conditioner and so the windows always had to be lowered. He usually parked it in his mechanic's compound because our compound, which was fenced in, had no entrance gate wide enough to allow his car into it.

One early Sunday morning, Uchenna, Edith and I had just returned from the spring, where we took our showers and fetched water for the household. As we entered the inner compound, my father was already dressed for church and was standing outside the house with a glass of water in his hand. He was to deliver the sermon that day at the St. Mary's Church, as he Periodically did (He was also a lay leader in church.) I had already walked past where he was standing but then a sudden and somewhat loud sound of the inner compound gate, slamming shut, caught my attention. I turned around and noticed that Mr. Eziuzo Nzewi, my father's car mechanic, had just hurriedly entered the compound. Sweat was streaming down his face and he was breathless! I was glued to where I stood, and my father asked Mr. Nzewi what had happened. In response, he asked, "Did you remove your car from my house today?" My father said no and added that he was in fact planning to pick up the car after church, to visit some family members. Mr. Nzewi then told him that his car was no longer where it was parked the previous night and he believed that it had been stolen. My father was very calm; he simply thanked him for letting him know and at that juncture, Mr. Eziuzo told him that he was going back to alert his neighbors, and so left hurriedly. Owning a car during and immediately after the war was almost a luxury. During the war, Biafran soldiers commandeered cars from civilians, stating that the vehicles were to be used in one way or the other to help prosecute the war. Many people were therefore happy to turn over their vehicles, because they felt it was the least they could do to help the war effort. After the war, those cars were not returned to their owners; many had been destroyed on the warfronts. The few cars left were rickety, but the owners guarded and cherished them jealously.

After thanking his mechanic for notifying him of what happened, my father walked into the house, told my mother what the mechanic said, picked up his bible and left for church. We all quickly followed in his footsteps, got ready and left for church.

That day in church, when it was time, my father delivered a masterful sermon, as he usually did. He made no mention of the car theft and no one listening to the sermon could have guessed that he had just lost a highly priced possession. It was after the sermon that the reverend in charge announced to the congregation that Mr. Uzokwe's car had just been stolen, amid gasps of *ewo-o-o*.

After the church, many family friends and well-wishers came to see him and offer their "condolences." Some immediately offered to form a search party. The police were called in and planning sessions for the search began in earnest. My father' friend, Mr. JBC Uzokwe, placed his car at the disposal of the search party and so began the search.

Two days later, the car was spotted near a town called Ekwuluobia, very close to where my father worked. The perpetrators were using it to ferry passengers along Ekwuluobia road. Once again, the police were informed and they came to our house. I remember my father being asked by one of the police men to give him the permission to shoot out the tires of the car, should they chance upon the thieves still driving it. My father quickly granted that request and they left. On the fourth day, the car was found, vandalized and abandoned along one of the dusty roads near Ekwuluobia. Again, even though we were bitter about the stealing of the car, it was seen as the direct result of the post-war suffering people were going through. The people who stole the car used it to ferry passengers to make money, which was exceedingly scarce at the time. Because of this, my father never expressed serious bitterness against them. I recall that he displayed the same attitude, during the war, when our food crops were uprooted prematurely by *Mpotimpo*.

As all these were happening, I could not hide the fact that I despised the federal troops, who were now occupying Nnewi in large numbers. They pranced around Nnewi as if they owned us. In the spring, where we fetched water, if you failed to let them fetch water before you, even though you got there before them, they would flog you. At the fuel station, if you failed to let them get fuel first, even though you were in line before them, they would flog you also. In the market, they would pick up whatever they need and then pay the owner whatever amount they felt like and the owner dared not protest. Their unruly behavior bothered me and I kept wondering how long the Igbos would be in that type of bondage. I was appalled by the actions of some Igbos, who seemed to immediately embrace the troops (or, should I say, "over-embrace" them). We derided a boy in my class who was said to be living with and running errands for some federal troops stationed in my village. We saw him as a traitor and called him all sorts of derogatory names like *"boy, aboki."* Benji Ibeanu, another classmate of mine, would stand up in class and demonstrate how the boy answered his master's calls. He would pretend he was a federal soldier giving orders to the boy and say, "*Aboki,* go fetch water, wash my clothes and serve my food," and then he would pretend as though he were the boy and answer, "Yes, sir," while jumping to attention. That was a very funny sight to behold; it provided comic relief to us, but for me, it provided more than that because I felt that the boy's parents were sellouts and so he deserved any denigration coming to him.

Benji Ibeanu was a very jovial boy; he had a slight speech impediment that caused him to pronounce "R" as "L" and vice versa. On the cover of a notebook he used for rough work, he wrote, "Lough Book," and I teased him immensely. Apparently, he wrote it the way he pronounced it. Benji later died a heart-breaking death. He came to school one day and had this very funny-looking boil right on top of his Adams apple. As usual, we started making fun of him just as he would make fun of anyone in that type of situation. We called him long throat and other names. Then as days went by, the boil broke and became an open sore. As before, the fun continued but after some weeks, this sore was still looking as fresh as it looked the very first time it opened. He was becoming self-conscious of it and had the tendency to cover it with his hand. Later, he started skipping school. This trend continued until he no longer showed up in school at all. We later heard that he had been taken to a specialist hospital in the town of Ibadan and we never heard from him again.

After what seemed like eternity had passed, one evening after school, I was playing soccer with other friends of mine at the St. Mary's Church football field when I heard someone call my name; it sounded like a female voice, but was faint. When I looked around the soccer field, I could not see any female, so I dismissed what I heard as my imagination—until I heard the voice again. I followed the direction it was coming from and sure enough, there was a woman standing on the road between Anglican Girls Nnewi and St. Marys Church; it was Benji's mother. She was carrying a type of basket we call *nkele ukpa* on her head with what seemed like personal belongings stashed inside it. I started walking towards her but she motioned to me not to come but simply said, "*Gwa nnegi na Benji anwuona*" or "Tell your mother that Benji has died." I was glued to the spot! All the muscles in my body froze and it seemed like I had temporarily lost control of them; I could hardly move. I then quickly scurried back to where the rest of the kids were still playing the soccer game and broke the news to them. While they were all going through the same type of shock, I ran home and told my mother what had happened and she let out a deafening shout of *ewo-o-o*. She knew Benji very well; he was always present at our *salaka* events when we prayed to God for the protection of Fidelis and Emmanuel. A couple of days later, the St. Mary's School pupils went to Benji's funeral at their house. As I watched him lying in a small wooden casket, I could not help but be imbued with an eerily overwhelming sense of sadness. This was a boy who used to be full of life and could make anyone laugh with his funny jokes. I continued to wonder why he succumbed to death after surviving the major scourges that the civil war threw at us.

At this time, a development that I found very ironic was occurring throughout eastern Nigeria; some of our young girls had started getting married to the federal soldiers! The girls were referred to as "*ndi gbaso ndi awusa*" or "people who went with Hausa." This infuriated many Igbos. We saw the girls as sellouts who would even marry people whose hands were soiled by the blood of their kinsmen. It became clear that they went after the soldiers because they needed money. I never thought of the fact that they were merely trying to survive; money was scarce in East Central State and the soldiers seemed to have it in abundance. The girls therefore felt that one way to get some of the money was by getting married to the soldiers. For their own part, some of the soldiers treasured being married to Igbo girls and treated the girls like "queens." Many of the marriages did not last very long; the villagers started to stigmatize the families of the errant girls, so some of them had a change of heart and returned to their homes. The stigma never really went away for those families.

School activities had intensified at this time and one day, at the St. Mary's School, the headmaster, Mr. P. Okeke, announced that General Yakubu Gowon was coming to the East Central State. I was surprised when he added that we were going to learn a song and sing in his honor in case he visited St. Marys! Was he insane? I wondered. How could we be singing a song in honor of a man that masterminded the tactical decimation of the Biafran nation? I felt that Mr. P. Okeke was out of his mind! But there was no way I could say what I felt because in those days teachers and headmasters still wielded enormous authority over children; they could assign corporal punishments, and if the child went home and complained, he would even be punished more by parents, for what they deemed as insubordination.

As the days went by, we started learning a standard song, which was said to have been prepared by all schools in the East Central State. The first time I heard the lyrics of the song, I was upset and infuriated; it went something like this:

We salute you, Gen. Gowon
Great Commander, you are welcome.
We are loyal, we are faithful,
Welcome, welcome to our State
By the Grace of God, we are one.

Imagine singing this song over and over as we were learning it. I could not hide my disdain for the teacher who was teaching the song. I thought to myself that he was a sycophant, like Mr. Ukpabi Asika. I used to like him as a person but now he was on the list of people I disliked.

General Gowon later visited the East Central state, but did not come to St. Mary's school and so we never had to sing that song for him; I was relieved. After the state visit, he donated bags of rice and cows to schools in the East Central State. St. Mary's School got our share of the rice and meat. On the last day of school, before we recessed for holiday, bigger girls and the female teachers started cooking the food. The cooking seemed to last all day. To pass time, the kids played soccer, netball, *oga* and *suwe*. As we played and waited, panic was suddenly whipped up in the school: a man whose face I still remember clearly, very fair in complexion and between twenty-two and twenty-four years old, rode into the school compound in a silver-colored Raleigh bicycle. At that moment, some male teachers were standing around, close to where we were playing. They were discussing issues related to the end of the term. The man on the Raleigh bicycle must have realized that they were teachers because he got down from his bicycle, steadied it by putting down the stand and then went directly to where they were standing. Any time a stranger came into the school compound, we always took notice and curiosity always led us to attempt to find out what the stranger wanted. I noticed that the man was sweating and looked edgy. When he got to the location where the male teachers were gathered, he introduced himself and—although I am not very certain about this, I think he called himself *Aguocha*. He told the teachers that he had just come from another school called *Egbo*. According to him, when the school finished cooking the food donated by General Gowon and distributed it to the pupils, the first kids that ate the food became very ill. He was insinuating that the food might have been poisoned! I did not need to hear more, the small crowd of kids that had now gathered unceremoniously dispersed in all directions.

As the news spread across the school compound, children started picking up their things and leaving. Uchenna was one of the people tasked with the responsibility of cooking; they were preparing the food at the back of the teachers' quarters. I immediately went to Edith, and before I could finish telling her what I just heard, she ran to her class, picked up her belongings and started towards home. I then headed to where Uchenna was cooking. As she saw me approach, she gave me a disapproving look. She just felt embarrassed that I was coming to where they were cooking. Boys had no business in the kitchen, lest "they would not grow beard." This was a saying that my mother effectively used in keeping the boys in my house out of the kitchen. She would also say that a man who goes to the kitchen often and learns how to cook very well never sustains a happy marriage, because, whatever the wife cooks, he will find faults with. Anyway, when I got to where Uchenna was, I composed myself as much as I could because she was the skeptic in the family; I knew that if I did not present my case convincingly, she would dismiss it. I told her what I had just heard and that most children were leaving and going home as a result. She just looked at me and laughed; she said they already heard the story but she did not believe it and was going to stay till the cooking was done. I could not believe what I was hearing, but knowing her as the skeptic of the family, there was no point trying to do any more convincing. She always had this self-assuredness about her; this singular quality earned her the nickname *Senior Agadi,* meaning senior elder, when she was at the Nnewi Girls Secondary School. I left the school compound and went home; when I got there, Edith was already home and had gone to narrate the story to my mother. To my surprise, my mother did not seem alarmed and was not worried that Uchenna was still at the school, cooking.

Some time late in the afternoon, Uchenna came back home; in her hand was a bowl of cooked rice and meat. Edith and I just watched her and wondered what she was up to next. She picked up a spoon and gradually started eating! She would eat one spoonful of rice and then scoop up another spoonful and stretch her hand towards our direction as if offering us some. Edith and I declined her offer. She continued this until she emptied that plate right before us! She then stood up, stretched and started rolling her eyes inwards as if she was about to pass out; a few seconds later, she closed her eyes keeled over. Edith and I were not sure what to make of all her antics; she was also the comic of the house and so we did not know if she was having any genuine problems or just pulling our legs. Just as I rose from where I was seated to approach her, she stood upright and burst out laughing.

17

Mama Goes to Onono

At the end of the war, after Emmanuel's return, hope once again soared in my mother's mind that Fidelis would come back from the war alive. That hope was too tempting to pass up; my mother felt that since God made it possible for Emmanuel to return safely, even after being cut off behind enemy lines in the war-torn town of Ohafia, he was also capable of doing the same in Fidelis' case. Every time word got to us that a Biafran soldier had returned from the war, we rejoiced for the person's family in the hope that very soon, it would be our turn. We longed for the day when others would join us in celebration of Fidelis' safe return.

Fidelis was one of those who believed strongly in the Biafran cause. After he joined the army, he rarely came back home to visit us. On the few occasions when he did, he was always itching to go back to the warfront immediately. During one of his visits, he was about to eat the food, which had been specifically prepared for him at my mother's behest, when a loud sound rocked the surrounding. He immediately sprang up from the chair and hurried outside, all the while asking, "What was that?" Just then, the sound of small arms fire followed. He rushed back into the house, asked that the food be removed, picked up his gun and started toward the door while muttering under his breadth, "It is Onitsha sector." He left and went back to Onitsha sector, where he was stationed.

My mother's anguish, as we continued to wait for Fidelis, never diminished her dedication to her patients. At this time, most people in Nnewi and surrounding areas had come to know her simply by her first name, Uzoma. By the time the war ended, the maternity home had burgeoned and blossomed and babies were being delivered at record levels.

One day, sometime after noon, a woman casually strolled into my mother's consulting room and made herself comfortable in a chair beside my mother. She had her medical chart, which the head nurse, Evelyn, had earlier completed in the waiting room. After reviewing her chart, my mother conducted the routine medical examination, but as she was about to write down the summary of her findings, the woman said to her, "*Mama, onwelu ife mcholu igwa gi*" ("Mama, there is something I want to tell you"). My mother described the look on the woman's face at that moment as serious. After years of practicing nursing and midwifery, my mother had come to earn the trust of many of her patients to the point that they expanded her role in their lives to include that of a family and marriage counselor. Some of them sometimes just came to confide in her about family problems, and then urged her to talk to their husbands, which she willingly did. As a result of this, when the woman lowered her voice and said she wanted to tell her something, my mother assumed that she was about to discuss some family matters. The woman cleared her voice, lowered it almost to a whisper and told her that a lady just came back from the town of Calabar in the southeastern part of Nigeria. She said that during a conversation in the market, the lady had said that my brother, Fidelis, was seen in Calabar. My mother could not believe what she was hearing. She asked who this lady was. The woman said she was not sure of her last name but gave a first name and added that she hailed from a village in Nnewi called Umudim. She was not sure where the lady's house was exactly in Umudim either. Since the woman seemed to know very little about the lady, my mother asked for a description of the lady's physical characteristics and where the conversation took place in the market. She then thanked the woman and gave her some money in appreciation.

My mother quickly and excitedly attended to the rest of the patients in the waiting room, and when she returned home from work that evening, she was bristling with happiness and hope as she told the story of her encounter to everyone, including my father. My father, being someone who never wore his emotions on his face, was sitting on his chair in the parlor and maintained a steady gaze towards the yard we called *mbalaezi*; he did not utter a word. I found it odd that my father did not seem to share in the enthusiasm and happiness we were all feeling. He simply sat still and listened to it all. At the end, my mother declared that she would be headed to Umudim first thing in the morning in search of the lady. My father did not object to her intended trip and simply wished her well.

The lack of specifics with respect to who the mystery lady from Calabar was and where she lived made the task of fishing her out in Umudim a tall order. My mother, however, was undaunted; she was determined to make the journey the next day to Umudim to begin the search. She contacted one Mr. Goddy Okoye, who is now deceased, to lead her to Umudim for the search. Goddy was very familiar with the village of Umudim. My father could not go with her because he had a crucial meeting in the town of Aguata, where he was the principal social welfare officer.

Anyone who is familiar with how villagers lived in Nnewi in those days will appreciate the enormity of the task ahead of my mother and Goddy Okoye. Then, Nnewi was not half as densely populated as it is today and people lived in compounds fenced in with mud or masonry block walls. The distance between the compounds, depending on locality, could sometimes run as much as a quarter of a mile. The walls of the perimeter fences were sometimes as high as the buildings inside; therefore, to communicate with someone in a compound, one had to physically go inside.

Such were the obstacles my mother and Goddy had to face when they arrived at the village of Umudim the next morning to begin the search. They went from compound to compound, asking whether there was any lady there who had just come back from Calabar. Of course, some of the families they met wondered what type of mission they were engaged in without ample information; others sympathized with her while politely telling her that they knew nothing about the elusive lady from Calabar. Some family members took time to narrate their own ordeal of relatives lost in the war. Some told encouraging stories of how they had given up hope about their relatives, only for the relatives to show up miraculously.

These mixed stories created an emotional roller coaster for my mother; at times she would become very hopeful after hearing the story of a miraculous return, but at other times, she would lose hope after hearing the tragic story of a loss. In the final analysis, by the time they visited the last compound in the area, she was very exhausted both physically and emotionally. Her feet were tired and sore. Her hope of finding the lady was dashed, but what did not diminish was her resolve to find Fidelis. That day, she left Umudim with disappointment and tears in her eyes but with hope that if Fidelis was indeed in Calabar, very soon, the God that brought back Emmanuel from Ohafia would also bring him back to Nnewi.

That morning, before my mother and Goddy left for Umudim, we had a family prayer and all wished her well before leaving for school. In school, my mind was preoccupied with a mixed bag of sentiments. Sometimes, a voice inside me would convince me that by the time we got back home from school my mother would already be back, armed with information she needed to go to Calabar and bring back Fidelis. At other times, something in me seemed to suggest that it might just be a wild goose chase, a feeling I did not like. I could not concentrate in class. I was in elementary four in Mr. Okonkwo, the bandmaster's class, along with people like Vicky Onwukwe, Nnamdi Okoye, Christian Onwuegbuna and Edwin Egwuatu. Every time I tried to concentrate on my schoolwork, Fidelis' image would appear in front of me, always dressed in camouflage, with a gun to match (this was how he was the last time we saw him). During recess, when all other kids had gone out to play soccer and other games, I quietly went to a corner, ruminating how all this would probably play out. I could not wait to leave when the dismissal bell finally rang. I ran back home from St Mary's Church, only to hear that my mother had not yet returned from Umudim—my heart sank! Edith came back later and was also disappointed. In my mind, the fact that my mother was still not back had an ominous connotation; if she had found the lady, why would she still be out there and not rush back home to break the good news? Is it possible that she found the lady and they both decided to rush down to Calabar to get

Fidelis? I continued to ponder this until much later in the evening, when she finally walked in with a very dejected look on her face. Right away, I knew that the journey was not a successful one. My worst fears had come to pass.

As she sat down and started narrating her ordeal, we were all disappointed; my father did not say much but just listened attentively, and every time my mother started sobbing, he would slightly look away. He returned his gaze to her only when she regained her composure and continued with the story. My heart was coming apart at the seams. I felt the anguish my mother was feeling, but my own personal anguish was increasing by the minute. When she finished her story, there was silence. No one seemed to know what to tell her, so one by one we started dispersing, and she was left in the parlor with my father.

When my mother later confronted the woman who led her on what we felt was a wild goose chase, she swore that the conversation she reported had really taken place in the market. She could not however provide further credible information about the whereabouts of the lady. Life continued in my family and my mother deeply immersed herself, as before, in her work at the maternity.

After the Umudim incident, the general consensus in our family was that if Fidelis were still alive, God would eventually bring him back to us. The Nigerian government was also adamant that there would be no reprisals against Biafran soldiers, so we were hopeful that Fidelis would return safely. We continued to hope, and before long another lady called *Agbala nko* appeared in my mother's maternity with the same type of story about Fidelis. This time, the woman said that some people from the Midwest came to her house the previous day and during a discussion, they said that one Fidelis Uzokwe, from Nnewi, was in a town, on the bank of the Niger River, called Onono. According to the woman, they said that Fidelis had removed his Biafran military uniform after the Nigerian troops overran the place and so had nothing to wear to come back to Nnewi. *Agbala nko* advised my mother to get some clothes together and hurry down to Onono for Fidelis. My mother was reluctant to pursue yet another rumor. She however felt that since she had known *Agbala nko* for some-time, if the story were false, she would not have the temerity to come to her with it. Also, she would have liked to verify the story first, but according to *Agbala nko*, the people had gone back to the Midwest. She therefore resolved to go to Onono, since it was close to Nnewi. Her optimism not withstanding, she did not know how to broach the news to my father, fear-ing that he would dissuade her from going to Onono because of her prior experience. When she came back that evening, she proceeded once again to tell the story of her encounter, but this time with measured and cautious optimism. She never sought endorsement about going to Onono; she just stated matter-of-factly, that she was going to Onono the next day. She asked for clothes from my father to take to Fidelis and my father obliged without any reluctance.

Very early the next morning, my mother rose and we all gathered for prayers; the prayer was that mama would have a safe journey to Onono and come back with Fidelis. We all wished her well and she was seen off as she set out for Onitsha, from where she would get to Onono by boat. Being from Asaba, which is close to Onono, my mother knew the general location of the town. The journey to Onitsha in a rickety vehicle, which she boarded at the Nnewi motor park garage, was not very pleasant. Being that this was her first time of traveling outside of Nnewi after the war ended, she had never seen the devastation that the war left behind. Along the roadside were charred vehicles and abandoned war machines, trees that had browned from the effect of guns and bombs. In some areas, human skulls and remains littered the landscape and every time she saw that, her thoughts quickly went to her father, brother and other relatives she had lost during the war. Intermittent cries and emotional outbursts characterized this journey, but she continued to hope that the return of her son would give her some comfort. When the vehicle got to Onitsha, she got off and had to trek the rest of the way to the Niger River bank from where she would be ferried over to Onono in a canoe. The Niger River bank was somewhat deserted except for a few fishing canoes drifting aimlessly on the river. She beckoned to a fisherman in one of the boats and when he came close, she asked if she could be taken to Onono. The man was puzzled and asked what she was going to Onono to do? She told him that she was going to bring back her soldier-son who was said to be there. The man shuddered and stated rather categorically that there were no Biafran soldiers at Onono. He said that all the Biafran soldiers captured in Onono by Nigerian soldiers were promptly transferred to Onitsha prison. He advised my mother to go and check the Onitsha prison before embarking on a journey he felt might turn out to be dangerous and fruitless.

She heeded the advice of the fisherman and walked back on foot into Onitsha, with the afternoon sun beating down mercilessly on her. As she asked for directions to the prison, she could feel her energy level already dwindling slowly. Her stomach was churning badly because, out of excitement, she did not get to eat before leaving that morning. By the time she got to the prison, she was sweating profusely.

Outside the prison stood a Nigerian army officer who sternly demanded to know what she was there for. She greeted him nicely and then told him what her mission was. As fate would have it, the soldier asked where she was from and she said Nnewi. The soldier said that the more he looked at her, the more she looked like someone from a family he used to know at Asaba. The soldier said he knew Maria Gwam. Maria Gwam is my mother's sister, who lived with us during the war and had just gone back to Asaba with Charles, Obiageli and *Mama Nnukwu*. My mother explained that she was from Asaba, but was married to an Nnewi man. She clarified to the soldier that Maria was her sister. This encounter completely changed the attitude of the soldier towards her. He motioned to a subordinate who had come closer on seeing him with my mother. He instructed the junior army officer to take my mother round the prison camp in search of Fidelis. Patiently, the soldier took my mother and they started going from prison camp to camp. In each section, they would stop and the soldier would demand the attention of the prisoners and then ask if Fidelis Uzokwe was in there. They went through all the sections and in each camp, the whole place fell silent as the soldier called out my brother's name. After going through the last camp, the soldier turned to my mother and sympatheti- cally said, "Well, this is the last camp and you can see that Fidelis is not here." Sensing the sympathy in his voice, my mother asked if they could go around one more time to see if anyone from Nnewi was in the camp. He obliged without objection and after the round, they could only find one young man who came forward and identified himself as an Okoye from a village called Edoji, in Nnewi. My mother asked if he had seen Fidelis and the young man said no. She then asked if his people knew that he was in Onitsha prison and he said no. My mother promised to pass word to his people that he was alive and well and at the prison. She thanked the soldier and the young man and started on the painful journey back to the bank of the River Niger. Beads of sweat were pouring down her body and she was becoming anxious.

Even though my mother had been told that there were no soldiers in Onono, she was not convinced; she was bent on going there to see things for herself, no matter the cost to her. She felt that her only hope of finding Fidelis lay in Onono. When she got to the bank of the river a second time, she beckoned on another fisherman in a boat who agreed to ferry her over to Onono, at a fee, but told her once again that she may not find anyone there. The canoe ride was not smooth; there were anxious moments when the boat seemed to tip to one side as if it would capsize. My mother con- tinually prayed that her trip in search of Fidelis would not result in a tragedy. It would be a taboo, she felt, for people to tell the story of a mother who drowned when she went in search of her son. Growing up in Asaba as a little girl, she used to swim, but thirty years had passed since she swam last. She did not feel that she would still be able to swim to safety in an emergency. The fisherman did not say a word to her but diligently paddled the canoe and even intensified his paddling efforts any time the canoe started tilting to one side. They got safely to Onono; there, she was dropped off in a very swampy and deserted area with trees all over. She could see a pathway, but there were no houses in sight. She noticed that the pathway was littered with burnt-out iron beds, trunk boxes and skeletal human remains. As the fisherman's boat started receding into the distance, her first instinct was to silently pray before starting out on the pathway to nowhere. As she walked, she tried to gauge whether the place was inhabited. There were very little signs to show that the place was currently inhabited but she could see destruction of lives and property all over. This did not daunt her, and she walked on. After a while, the pathway widened and in the distance she could see a small, dilapidated building right in the middle. She made for the small house and as she got closer, two men in military uniforms materialized from the building and fixed their gaze on her. Her heart started racing; she was wondering how the soldiers would react to her problems. When she got to the house, she greeted them, but was too frightened to tell them what she came for because of the looks in their eyes. She just told them that she was looking for her mother, who was left in Onono at the outset of the war. One of the soldiers promptly told her that her mother was not there but directed her to a shack, which was about half a mile away and said that there was a family there and she could go and ask them. She thanked them nicely, turned and headed for the shack.

At this time, judging from what she saw, hope that she would find Fidelis in Onono was beginning to dim; she could tell that fierce fighting may have taken place there, but Fidelis could not possibly be there. As she approached the shack, she saw a man sitting in front, directly facing a body of water; he was mending a fisherman's net. Just as she started speaking to the fisherman, a pregnant woman and a young boy came out of the shack. She greeted them all and narrated her ordeal. When she finished her story, the man did not mince words in telling her that all the captured soldiers had been sent to Onitsha prison. The man added that he would not see a Biafran soldier trapped there, just because of lack of clothes, and not do something; instead, he would remove the clothes he had on his body, give them to the soldier to wear and go. At this point, a mother's hope was crushed! My mother knew that she had no other hope to hope against.

When Fidelis was not found in Onitsha prison, she still had hope because she had not come to Onono yet, but this time, there was nothing else to hope against. She broke down and cried. The fisherman's family consoled her as much as they could. When she regained her composure, the man asked where she was from and my mother told him. The boy excitedly said he went to school at St. Mary's during the war because his family sought sanctuary in Nnewi. He asked if my mother knew St. Mary's School and headmaster Odunukwe, and she said yes. Mr. Odunukwe was the headmaster at the St. Mary's primary school during the war and I believe he was even there before the war started. Once again they empathized with my mother, and then it was time for her to leave. All the time that she was making her way to Onono, she did not succumb to fear, even when she went by the destruction littered all over the landscape. However, with her last hope having evaporated into thin air, she could no longer manage her fear; suddenly, she felt like she could no longer walk by the pathway to go back to the river bank. Bad thoughts started creeping into her mind, she thought about the skeletal remains all over the landscape and wondered what may have happened to Fidelis. The thought was simply too much to bear. She stated her fear to the fisherman who asked the little boy to escort her to the riverbank. At the riverbank, my mother thanked the boy and as he left, she found herself speaking out loudly, addressing Fidelis. These were her words: "Fidelis, if you are still alive, please return. I have traveled far and wide to search for you, to no avail. My feet are tired and sore and my mind is weak. I can no longer go on. If you are no longer living, I assure you that in my next lifetime, I will be your mother again, because you made me proud. God speed you." At this time, her face was drenched with tears. She let loose all the emotions that had been building up in her; she cried until her eyes dried out on their own.

As she was washing off her face, she heard the swishing sound of a fishing canoe nearby. When she raised her head, a canoe was approaching, so she beckoned on the fisherman and he picked her up and ferried her into Onitsha. From there, she walked to Ochanja market. She was now so exhausted that she was walking in measured steps. The sun was beginning to set and market people had gradually begun to gather their things to head home. In the market, she met a lady from Nnewi called Mrs. Felicia Nnadi. She asked my mother what she had come to do. Not comfortable discussing her ordeal, she simply told the lady that she had gone to Asaba to see her people and was now on her way back home to Nnewi. The lady said she was also heading back to Nnewi, but my mother knew that in traveling back with her, she might break down and talk about her ordeal. She therefore said she still had some business to attend to in Onitsha, and the two women went their separate ways.

Dusk was already gathering when my mother returned that evening. Before she came back, concern about her own safety was already reaching a feverish pitch. I was already blaming my father in my mind for not suspending his work for that day and taking my mother to Onono in his car. I felt that he put his work ahead of the interest of the family. I began to wonder why he did not seem to be actively participating in the process of searching for Fidelis.

Earlier in school on that day, I could not concentrate, but during recess I tried to occupy my time with soccer. I was more optimistic about the journey because my mother had argued that since she knew *Agbala nko*, she would not tell her the story if it were not true. I kept counting the minutes, hoping for school to be over while my imagination ran wild. How tall would Fidelis be now, I wondered? Would he be as lean as Emmanuel was when he came back from Ohafia? Would he go back to Merchants of Light School again, or go to another school?

My mother narrated the story of her journey and the whole family was very emotional about it; amidst sobbing and crying, she finished her story and then stated rather strongly that she would no longer embark on these journeys again. She said that Fidelis would find his father's compound from which he left for the war. Apparently, *Agbala nko* had deceived a vulnerable woman and sent her on a wild goose chase that could have ended her life.

After that episode, I continued to wonder what people gain from preying on the vulnerable. My brother Fidelis did not go to the war to fight for Uzokwe family, he went to fight for Biafra, and for any Biafran to have sadistically sent my mother running around, often under difficult and dangerous situations in search of Fidelis, was the height of callousness.

18

Fidelis' Funeral

My mother was never formally told by anyone that Fidelis had been killed, so throughout the duration of the futile and gut-wrenching wait she was hopeful that God would somehow come through for us. Even after her journey to Onono, when she vowed never to embark on more forlorn trips in search of my brother, she still held out hope that he would be in one of Nigeria's prison camps. In our house, she made sure that the items that belonged to him were carefully preserved, as if to ensure that whenever he returned he would know that we never gave up on him.

As for my father, as much as he felt that the trance-like dream he had about the demise of Fidelis was real, he had no concrete or first-hand information to make him declare that the wait was over. He therefore did not discourage my mother from going on those trips. In fact, he later admitted that he was also hoping for a miracle and prayed silently for one every time my mother went in search of Fidelis. The kids in our house were not sure what to think. As the months went by, I developed a pattern of periodic restlessness in my sleep; I would dream about Fidelis and wake up with actual tears in my eyes and then feel sad for the better part of the morning. I must confess that I am still sensitive about issues relating to the Biafran war and the senseless loss of lives. Passage of time does not seem to have made a very big difference for me.

As the months went by, one could sense that the intensity of my mother's optimism was no longer waxing as strong as it was when the war initially ended. Some days, in her prayers, she seemed to forget to mention my brother's name as she customarily did before then. On other days, she would simply say, "Lord, please be with Fidelis, wherever he is." This continued until one day in 1972, about two years after the war ended. She woke up from what she described as a troubled sleep and called my father into her room. When he joined her, she asked him to sit down and then attempted to say something, but the words would not come out; instead, tears welled up in her eyes and she was overcome with emotions. She wept while my father, who was confused at this time as to what the problem was, tried to console her. When she regained her composure, she said to my father, "*Ozugo, Fide anwugo,*" meaning, "It is enough. Fide is dead." My father was befuddled because he had carefully stopped bringing up the issue of Fidelis whenever she was around, to avoid upsetting her. She then told my father that she was in a dream and Fidelis, looking very somber, appeared to her and said, "*Mama, enirom ofuma,*" or "Mama, I was not properly buried." She ended by saying that it was a final sign to her that her son was no longer alive; she stated that she was now ready to offer his last funeral rites and put the whole episode in the past. As she spoke, teardrops were streaming down my father's face, and he occasionally looked away to dab the tears; but after a while he could no longer contain his emotions, so he let go, openly broke down and wept. He then told my mother about the trance-like dream he had during the war when he was told that Fidelis had been killed. He said that he was so convinced that the dream was real that he put Fidelis' soul in God's hands thereafter. He told my mother that the heart palpitations he developed was the result of the many sleepless nights he had after the dream, and that the irritability some of us noticed in him was the direct result of the dream. He said that the agony multiplied because he could not share his feelings with us for fear of whipping up alarm. He told her how he heard an innuendo that Fidelis may have been killed, but the source had also gotten the information second hand and he could not corroborate it. He concluded by saying that, in spite of all that, his belief in God and biblical miracles made him harbor some hope that Fidelis may just come walking in one day. He cited the case of one of the Biafran soldiers, in Nnewi, whose funeral had already been held, but who came back after several months, as another reason why he held out some hope. From that day on, my parents began to openly acknowledge that Fidelis had passed on and the prayers changed to, "Lord, accept his soul."

After this incident, I began to recall all the actions and reactions from my father when my mother went on the futile trips in search of Fidelis. It became clear why he did not display as much optimism as the rest of us when we were told that my brother was spotted in Onono and Calabar. I remembered wondering why he seemed so cold and always looked away whenever my mother narrated the story of her journey.

As for me, thirty-three years after that horrendous war, I still feel very sad when I remember my brother. I think that the pain is exacerbated by the fact that there is no grave for him. It is possible that if his remains were brought home and buried, maybe I would have had some semblance of closure. Sometimes, I feel a searing pain shoot through my heart when I remember that he still lies elsewhere; it makes me feel like we have not done for him everything he would have done for us if the situation were reversed. Also, the absence of a grave makes me sometimes view him as someone who went on a journey and is yet to return, and that unfortunately seems to keep the wound in my heart fresh and prolongs the anguish. On several instances over the years, I have caught myself daydreaming that he may still walk through our gates, but I know that, in reality, he is gone forever.

I have often sought to find Biafran war veterans who may have witnessed or have first hand information about how and where Fidelis died. My intent is just to ask the common question which families of fallen soldiers ask: "Did he suffer?" I do not know what this would do for me, but deep down I am hoping to hear, "No, he did not suffer; he died as soon as he was hit." Maybe that would reduce the agony I feel and convince me that my brother is resting in peace.

We have heard all manners of rumors since then; some said he was killed in Onitsha sector one November evening after one of the fiercest fights Biafra waged to preclude Onitsha from falling into enemy hands. It was said that a lot of Biafra's best also fell by the bullet that night. They said that the mortar landed too close for anything to have been done for him. Some even told us that his men retrieved his remains and buried him with full military honors in Oba. This part I find difficult to fathom because, as an officer, why would they bury him just a few miles from his town, Nnewi, without parental or family notification? If they could get him to Oba, why could they not get him to Nnewi, a few more miles away?

When my father passed away at age seventy-three in 1992, he still carried the scar of my brother's death. He never really got over it; little things made him remember Fidelis and he made references to his bravery and selflessness every now and then. Fidelis held a lot of promise before the cruel hand of death snatched him away at the prime of his youth, but regardless of that, during his short-lived existence, he made the Uzokwe family and Biafra proud.

He was a very brave boy with an equally gentle soul. This was exemplified in what he did when his friend, Joe Agbasi was killed in the war. He came home in full military camouflage with a gun he called setima. He went to Joe's funeral and released several gunshots into the air as a tribute to a fallen friend; he then went into the room where Joe's grieving mother was and offered his condolence. He told her to take heart that Joe did not die in vain but for a good cause. He then proceeded to ask her to take him as a son and promised that he would do for her everything Joe would have done. That was vintage Fidelis; a friend in need and a friend indeed. It was sad that he never lived to actualize his promise to Joe's mother, but two very good friends died fighting for a cause they strongly believed in.

If Fidelis really died fighting in Onitsha sector, I am sure he would have had no regrets. Onitsha is a town he loved so much; it was the town where Aunt Mamaocha made her living for many years and where Fidelis visited her frequently on holidays. At the time of aunt Mamaocha's passing in 1997, at age 87, she still fondly remembered him and speculated about what he might have become, had he lived.

His funeral was finally held in 1974, four full years after the tragic war ended. It took that long because my family could not let go. At first, the thought of a funeral ceremony was too difficult to bear; it would mean that Fidelis was gone forever and we were not ready to accept that; it would mean that there was no hope to hope against anymore.

On that eerily gloomy day, there was no casket to behold or pay final respects to, there was no grave to mark the final resting place of the Biafran hero. Even his eulogy was not complete because the date of his death was not known. The sun came up early that day, but as people slowly assembled, the clouds began to gather and eventually cast an ominous haze over the horizon. It was symbolic to many and to me; the sun had set for the last time for a gallant soldier; the sun had set for a boy who gave it his best shot, just like all fallen Biafran heroes. One thing remained clear: even four years after the war, many still came to honor him. Most of his friends died in the same conflict, but the few remaining ones paid their respect in a manner befitting a war hero. At a point during the funeral ceremony, my father picked up his double-barrel gun and slowly walked over to the end of the compound, away from the crowd. He aimed his gun at the fronds of a palm tree and let off a couple of shots as a tribute to a son he would always be proud of. Barely in class two in secondary school that year, I contributed my widow's mite by designing lettered graphics, which were put close to his picture and read: *Here is the hero, Fidelis Ikechukwuka (Dike) Uzokwe.*

It was clear from the attendance at Fidelis' funeral that many still missed him. The threatening cloud did not deter them. When the bell tolled for the final time, my mother opened up and cried; we all cried together for Fidelis. He was a gift from God but was taken away prematurely.

Even though I agonize that the war was ever fought to the detriment of many families in Biafra, one song by the St Mary's choir constantly reminds me of why Fidelis, Emmanuel and countless other Biafrans went to war. The song reminds me why I should no longer agonize over the death of my brother. The song registers the astonishment of a mother when her son who went to fight for Biafra came back home, but without his two arms. The name of the Biafran soldier was Okechukwu. The song goes thus in my native dialect:

Okechukwu nwam inata, Okechukwu, nwa jel'agha
Ma keduzi akagi nabo iji akwa mgbo?
Keduzi akagi nabo iji eli nni?
Keduzi akagi nabo, Chukwu nyelu gi?

Ewo-o, mama –o, nnem –o, papa m-o, nna-a
Oyim-o, umunnem, unu ebezilinam akwa, biko

Kama Hausa g'ekpochapu Biafra
Akam jebe
Ukwum jebe
Isim jebe
Ndum jebe
Obu aja nke mchuru Biafra

Okechukwu nwam, Okechukwu nwam, Okechukwu nwam inatago
Ewo, Okey, ewo, Okey mo-o
O, biko umunnem, umunem, ndi Biafra
Kanyi kenenu Okechukwu, Odogwu n'agha
Odogwu Biafra.

meaning:

Okechukwu, my son, are you back, Okechukwu, my son that went to war.
But where are the two hands you used to man your gun?
Where are the two hands you used to eat?
Where are the two hands God gave you?

Ewo-o, my mother, my mother, my father, my father,
My friends, my brethren, do not cry for me

Instead of allowing the Hausas to annihilate Biafra
Let my hands go,
Let my legs go,
Let my head go,
Let my life go,
It is a sacrifice I made for Biafra

O, please my brethren, Biafrans
Let us thank Okechukwu, the war hero
Biafra's hero

This song captures the situation in Biafra as well as the disposition of many Biafran soldiers during the war. It always evokes a certain amount of emotionalism every time I remember or sing it. It is as relevant to me today as it was thirty-three years ago, when the VOBR first sang it.

The part of the song that touches me most is where Okechukwu asked his brethren not to cry for him because his misfortune was a sacrifice made for Biafra. He then states that instead of allowing the northerners to annihilate Biafra, he was ready to lay down his life. That is the same position my brother took; he paid the ultimate price so that Biafrans like me would live. Our children and our children's children will therefore continue to pass this story from one generation to another for posterity. It has already started because on September 16, 2002, my son, Alfred Jr., who is a 9th grader, made a PowerPoint presentation to his classmates about the Nigeria-Biafra war. His account was based mainly on information he gathered from Internet research.

This book has been very therapeutic for me—it has helped me to unburden my mind and find some semblance of closure to the Biafran experience. The emails I got from Nigerians from all over the world when I released some excerpts of this book on Nigeriaworld website gave me a glimpse into the minds of many Nigerians of Biafran extraction. Many are suffering in silence about their experience and the losses they had to endure during the war. Many lost fathers, many brothers, many uncles and many more. A boy who lost his father (a very prominent physician) during an air raid in Aba told me how his family was turned upside down by the experience. He was a child then, but went through the experience of growing up and imagining what it was like to have a father. In my responses to the people who emailed me, I gave them this advice: unburden your minds by talking about it and somehow, closure would follow.

In ending, I would borrow a leaf from my mother and say that in my next world, Fidelis Ikechukwuka will be my brother again. **Adieu, Fide.**

My mother, left, with one of her patients in her consulting room after the war. This was the same place Agbala nko told her the rumor that sent her to Onono.

1973-my mother in front of Uzoma Maternity Home

My mother delivered the quadruplets above immediately after the war, at Uzoma Maternity Home.

1975-Ezengozi (left) and Emmanuel (right) in Asaba during the funeral service of my grandfather, G.W. Gwam.

1970—Nnamdi (left) and me (right). Boy Scouts continued even after the war.

1981—my father in Chicago, Illinois.

1997—Ijeoma, Boston, Massachusetts

1981—with my father in Chicago Illinois

1997—Edith, Boston, Massachusetts

2001—Baltimore, Maryland, Emmanuel (left), Nnamdi and me (right)

1996—King of Prussia, Pennsylvania, my mother.

1999—with my kids, from left, Lilian, Jennifer, Chris, Sylvanus. Alfred Jr. in the back.

EPILOGUE

Ojukwu Returns from Exile

At the end of the war in January of 1970, when Nigerian soldiers entered my hometown Nnewi, one of the first moves they made was to occupy the house built by Sir Odumegwu Ojukwu, the father of Biafra's leader, Col. Chukwuemeka Ojukwu. Located in Umudim, Nnewi, the house was a modest bungalow with a raised foundation. Anyone who may have heard about the considerable wealth and influence of Sir Odumegwu Ojukwu may not immediately be impressed by the outward appearance of the house; they might be expecting to see an opulent mansion, decked out with all types of ornaments, befitting the first African millionaire. It was, however, my understanding that the exterior of the house was extremely deceiving.

Nonetheless, Nigerian soldiers strategically positioned an armored tank in the compound, with the barrel of the gun pointing towards the entrance gate. I was always amused by the presence of the armored tank every time I passed by the compound. It seemed as though the Nigerian soldiers were guarding the house in case the Biafran leader decided to parachute into the compound some day and start the quest for Biafra anew; it was silly. One of the rumors in Nnewi at the time was that after the death of Sir Odumegwu Ojukwu in the mid sixties or so, his body was embalmed and placed in an elaborately designed and accessible tomb in his compound in Nnewi. It was said that when Col. Ojukwu was about to leave Biafra in 1970, he had to make a special but quick trip to Nnewi to pick up the embalmed body, which he carried along with him to Ivory Coast. I doubt the veracity of the embalmed body story, but it always got me thinking: I wondered what the federal troops, who were at this time marauding Nnewi, would have done to the embalmed body had Col. Ojukwu left it behind. Judging from the barbaric way they were behaving in Nnewi at the time, I felt that they could possibly have tried to exact revenge on a dead body through desecration or other such means. These soldiers were wild; they used every opportunity to show the civilian population that they were in charge; they roamed around, issuing orders to civilians, enticing and seducing our young women folk with money and commandeering young boys to do chores for them. It was unbelievable!

One example of their tyrannical behaviors still stands out in my mind. We started a marching band at the St. Mary's School; I was a member of the band and after an all elementary school contest at Nkwo Nnewi, we placed second, behind St. Stephen's school, Umudim. To celebrate our victory, the band was visiting the homes of some prominent dignitaries like Chief Z.C.Obi, Chief Ejike Chidolue and others. What we essentially did was to go to their house and play our music, after which they gave us some money, which we hoped to use for upgrading the school band. As we moved from house to house, other kids were flocking after us.

We had just finished playing in Chief Z.C. Obi's compound near Anglican Girls Secondary School Nnewi and were about to cross the highway to the other side of the road, when an open-bodied army land rover was spotted speeding from the Onitsha side of the highway towards the direction of Nkwo market. Sensing that the vehicle, which was occupied by soldiers, was not slowing down, the bandmaster frantically motioned to all band members to stay put on the other side. Just then, a little boy in the crowd attempted to cross the road and the next thing we heard was a loud bang! The boy was hit by the vehicle. The impact knocked him off the pavement, but he quickly fell back and blood was all over the place. The vehicle came to a screeching halt and one of the soldiers quickly came down and without saying a word to anyone, picked up the boy, climbed up the vehicle and sped off. It turned out that the boy was Chibueze Egemonye; their house was just in the vicinity. The scene that was vividly etched in my mind was when the boy's sister, Uju Egemonye, started crying and saying "*Okwanu Chibueze-o-o,*" meaning, "It is Chibueze." What struck me most was that the driver never even tried to ascertain who the parents or family of the boy were. The soldiers felt that they could do what they wanted without accountability. Also, the fact that the driver saw the teeming crowd of mainly children along that road should have been a good reason to slow down or stop momentarily, but again he felt that he could do whatever he wanted and go scot-free. The good news is that Chibueze survived the accident, although I do not know the details of what transpired later. This type of behavior by the soldiers continued to infuriate me.

Things continued to chug along and in 1973 I became a freshman in secondary school; my school was located within walking distance from Ojukwu's residence. In school, I was posted to a hostel named after Sir Odumegwu Ojukwu and I loved it because the reverence I had for the Biafran leader was still undiminished. The hostel was reputed as the best in the school in almost every facet of school life; most of the students in the hostel did very well in the West African School Certificate Examination and every Saturday, when hygiene inspections of hostels were conducted, Ojukwu house was always on top. I was beginning to feel that everything associated with the Biafran leader had an air of superiority to it.

Later, a boy named David Ojukwu, who was somewhat burly in physique, joined our school and was posted to Ojukwu house. He told us that he was Col. Ojukwu's nephew. He also said he spent the war years in London. It was always mesmerizing as the rest of us: Obumneme Okeke, Samuel Nnoli, Tagbo Ike, Abuchi Okafor, Moses Nwosu, Chukwuma Okonkwo and more would sit around and listen to the boy tell stories about his family; he would refer to Col. Ojukwu as "Emeka," creating the impression that he was very close to the Biafran leader. I always envied him and wished I were as close as he said he was to Ojukwu.

Years after the war, many Igbos still wished for Ojukwu's return from exile; my father would always remember him in prayers and ask God to continue to guide him where he was. This continued until sometime in 1982; Ojukwu had been in exile for about twelve years and Nigeria had become a democracy. Alhaji Shehu Shagari was the president and another round of election was coming up. We started hearing rumors that plans were afoot to pardon Ojukwu and bring him back from exile; we were all exhilarated at the prospect of having our undisputable and brave leader back in our midst. However, some people speculated that Alhaji Shehu Shagari had no powers to pardon him; they surmised that such a move could give the military men, who would see Ojukwu's pardon as an affront on them, a reason to come back to power. This issue became a subject of daily debate in the nation as well as on the campus of University of Nigeria, where I was putting finishing touches to my thesis project. Speculations were rife; people wondered what he would do if and when he eventually returned from exile. Some said he had become so wealthy and comfortable in Ivory Coast that he could not just uproot and return to Nigeria; they felt that if he were pardoned, he would just come back briefly to acknowledge the pardon and then return to Ivory Coast, which was now his base. These speculations continued until the day an official announcement was made to the effect that he was pardoned and was free to return to Nigeria. The whole campus and indeed the eastern states were agog with anticipation and celebration. One thing that I found very intriguing about this whole issue was that his pardon seemed to be welcomed, at least in my school, by students of all ethnicities, Yorubas and others. Many of my Yoruba friends and classmates, including my girlfriend, Bukola, were eager to see him return. Students brought in pictures of Ojukwu, which he had taken in exile, into the campus and pasted them all over. As usual, in those pictures, he looked very healthy and did not seem to have been worn out by life in exile.

On the day Ojukwu was supposed to return, I drove to Enugu airport with my classmate Ikegbunam Anya and my girlfriend Bukola. It was only a couple of miles away. When we got to the airport, we were unprepared for the crowd that had gathered, also awaiting Ojukwu's arrival. Some people climbed onto trees, walls and any raised objects, just to catch a glimpse of the war hero. When his plane touched down, I believe that the first dignitary to alight from the aircraft was Dr. Chuba Okadigbo, who was a member of the National Party of Nigeria and was said to have helped broker the final pardon deal. After a short wait, the Biafran leader stepped out of the airplane. Instantaneously, a thunderous ovation erupted from the thousands that had gathered. I could remember Bukola muttering, "The man is an enigma." People were falling over one another just to catch a glimpse of him.

After acknowledging greetings from the crowd, he climbed into a sun-roof Mercedes Benz car, stood upright and as he waved to the crowd, the car started its slow but triumphant entry into the Igbo heartland. It was a highly symbolic moment for all Igbos regardless of their political affiliation. Biafra was not dead after all; the symbol of Biafra was making a triumphant entry back into the city, Enugu, where the struggle had begun about sixteen years earlier. It was a very joyous occasion and we all took it in with patriotic fervor.

We had already been told that the then governor of Anambra State, Jim Ifeanyichukwu Nwobodo, had organized a reception for the Biafran enigma and we were expecting that Ojukwu and his entourage would be stopping by the state house, which was on his way, to pay a courtesy call on the governor. Jim Nwobodo belonged to a different party, the Nigerian People's Party (NPP), and even though NPP was not the party in power at the federal level, and therefore was not responsible for the pardon of Ojukwu, we all felt that his return was an Igbo affair. All political differences and bickering were therefore to be set aside for that day by all Igbos to savor the epoch-making moment. When Ojukwu's entourage left the Enugu airport, it took a while before the crowd dispersed and we finally left the airport and headed back to the campus. We were collectively surprised when we heard later that day that Ojukwu and his entourage bypassed the governor's mansion at the Independence layout, effectively snubbing the governor, and headed for Nnewi. I have never been a fan of Governor Jim Nwobodo, having attended one of his numerous statehouse parties with my classmate, Mike Ukoha and Bukola and seen the lavishing of government money. I was however sure that Governor Nwobodo had prepared the reception for Ojukwu, out of reverence for the former eastern region leader and genuine Biafran hero who once occupied the state house. This was the same reason why thousands gathered at the Enugu airport to welcome him. It was disconcerting for many in the campus that Ojukwu snubbed the governor. We wondered if those who granted him pardon were not cowing him into repudiating his kinsmen. As for me, I wondered if he had forgotten that he was THE Igbo leader, whose love for and dedication to his people should transcend party lines. This singular incident would bother me for days, and as we all discussed this in the campus it became clear that very many Igbos, even those who had no liking for Governor Jim Nwobodo, found that action untoward, especially coming from THE Igbo leader. A lot of conjecture was thrown around in school as to what informed Ojukwu's actions; some said that he may have signed a pact with the people that pardoned him to snub members of other parties, Igbo or not, so as to give NPN some political advantage. Just before we could recover from the shock about the snubbing of Governor Nwobodo, another shocker hit—it was reported that Ojukwu did not stop by to encourage Biafran war heroes at Oji encampment! Oji encampment is a camp where many Biafran soldiers who sustained very incapacitating injuries during the war were herded for reasons I still do not understand. Oji is located along Enugu/Onitsha road and is just a few miles away from Enugu. On hearing that their erstwhile leader was coming their way, the incapacitated soldiers, some confined to wheel chairs while others walked with the aid of crutches, lined up along Enugu/Onitsha road to catch a glimpse of him. Of course we all expected that Ojukwu would make a brief stop there to offer them some words of encouragement. When we heard that he did not go in to see these soldiers, a symbolic gesture that would have meant a lot to all Igbos, we were disappointed to the core. This was especially painful to me as someone who had lost many people during the war. That incident, to an extent, diminished the reverence I had for my hero. Even my father, who was so enamored by Ojukwu that he would have done anything Ojukwu asked for, was disappointed.

From then on, a chain of activities, which further put Ojukwu at odds with some of the people he stood up for during the war, took place. He officially joined the National Party of Nigeria and started openly supporting Alhaji Shehu Shagari for re-election! Many people have argued that the real reason he snubbed Nwobodo was because of the fact that Dr. Nnamdi Azikiwe was the flag-bearer of Jim Nwobodo's party, Nigerian Peoples Party. Dr. Nnamdi Azikiwe, of course, defected from Biafra into Nigeria during the war, thereby diminishing the resolve of most Biafrans. Some said that Ojukwu had not forgiven him for that and used the opportunity of his return from exile to pay him back in his own coin. That is perfectly understandable because many of us were still bitter about Azikiwe's crossover, also. But it is my feeling that if Ojukwu had completely abstained from politics, thereby making himself a non-partisan Igbo man who would represent Igbo interest no matter the person's political affiliation, he would have probably become the undisputable voice of the Igbo race till this day. It is true that he is still one of the leaders of the Igbos today, but he is no longer THE supreme voice of the Igbos. This is even evident in the fact that when Ojukwu entered for the senatorial race for Onitsha zone, immediately after his return from exile, he lost to a little-known small-time politician called Edwin Onwudiwe. This also went a long way in eroding or diminishing the myth that had, before then, surrounded the enigma that was Ojukwu. Many Igbos found him vulnerable at the time and a floodgate of attacks on him, some of which I found unfair at the time, opened. Even some Biafran commanders who had served under him joined in the criticism. It was very troubling.

To this day, some people argue that joining the NPN party may have been one of the conditions of Ojukwu's pardon; they reason that the pardon may have been revoked had he decided to back out. To that I say, Ojukwu should have stood on principle, just like Mandela did, and would have remained an Igbo icon, even in exile.

Ojukwu has gradually warmed his way back into the hearts of many Igbos, including me. He is not just an Igbo man to me; he is an Igbo man from my hometown who prevented the attempted destruction of a people. A man who staked his well being, his life and his father's considerable wealth to stave off the annihilation of his people; that is admirable and has gone down in history. As I was writing this section of the book, an email came to me from one of the readers of my column on Nigeriaworld.com. He was responding to my commentary about the quest for Igbo presidency in Nigeria. He wrote that if the Igbos want to have a president of Igbo extraction in Nigeria, they must wash their hands of Ojukwu. I responded that the Igbos could never and would never distance themselves from Ojukwu. The name Ojukwu has become synonymous with the Igbo race by dint of the fact that he stood up for us when it all mattered. He therefore remains a hero for this generation of Igbos and those to come.

Igbos and the Biafran war

The civil war left a lot of bitterness in Igbos as a people; but why not? Their villages were ravaged by air raids, thousands of their children died of *kwashiorkor*, their population was rendered homeless and had to move from town to town in search of sanctuary while their sons, uncles and husbands met their untimely deaths on the warfronts. In any civilization, war brings about change, sometimes positive and sometimes negative, but in most cases, the changes tend to assume a survivalist dimension, where people affected by it position themselves to counter or minimize the effect of such conflicts, should they reoccur. The Biafran war is not an exception; many changes have occurred within the Igbo community since the end of the war, and while not all can be directly attributed to the war experience, several can be traced to it. Most of the changes are geared towards ensuring that a reoccurrence will not be as devastating as before. This chapter discusses some of the changes I observed since the conflict ended thirty-three years ago.

Housing

In this book, I narrated how in 1966 some of the Igbos who returned to their respective hometowns in eastern Nigeria, to escape the pogroms in the North, faced biting housing problems. They had no houses of their own in their hometowns; yet, they used to live in mansions in the townships where they worked prior to the war. The situation was so bad that some had to "room in" with their relatives in crowded houses, and in some instances, ancillary buildings were converted into living quarters to house the returnees. Also, as Egyptian pilots started bombing civilian targets all over Biafra, rendering many families homeless, the housing problem worsened. Refugees had to be housed in open elementary school buildings. They slept on bare floors, ate whatever they could gather and suffered all manner of diseases, resulting in many untimely deaths. This problem persisted throughout the war period.

Igbos seem to have learned a very important lesson about housing from that war experience. Immediately after the war, as soon as they were able to re-establish their footings financially and otherwise, they reversed the pre-war trend of building houses in the townships and neglecting their hometowns. These days, many build family houses in their hometowns first, before doing so wherever they live and work. To them, the saying that charity begins at home has taken an added significance; it is not uncommon to find an Igbo family of about five, domiciled in a city like Lagos, building a twelve-room mansion in the East. The irony though, is that the houses in the villages are seldom used; some spend as little as four weeks in a year in those houses, yet, as one family told me, they would rather have too many rooms in their family house because "tomorrow is pregnant." Igbos living in the Diaspora have joined the bandwagon; they send money to their relatives in their respective hometowns in eastern Nigeria, for the construction of family houses for them. As I stated before, although all this trend cannot be directly attributed to the war experience, it has a lot to do with it.

In the unlikely event of another conflict, many want to have a comfortable place to run to. Discretion, they say, is the better part of valor.

Employment in Eastern states

Unemployment was another huge problem experienced by Igbos when they returned to the eastern region in 1966. The eastern region, which was mainly populated by civil servants, especially Enugu, had very few industries and other facilities that would have provided employment for the returnees. I recall that when my family returned to Nnewi, my mother went to Enugu to look for work as a nurse and midwife. After registering with the government and being told that she would be called later, the call never came. It was this experience that motivated her into establishing Uzoma Maternity Home, Nnewi. However, it must be stated here for the record that, judging from the number of easterners displaced from the North and South who had to return to the East, it would have taken a miracle to completely resettle them and provide employment for all. All the same, the employment problem then opened the eyes of some Igbos to the merits of investing some of their money in the eastern states.

When the war ended, some Igbos stayed back in the eastern states and nurtured very successful businesses. They built and ran successful industries, schools, hospitals and other job-producing ventures. As I write, these ventures have proliferated to an unprecedented level, providing employment in the areas. In Nnewi alone, there are many successful industries, schools, hospitals and business concerns established by the indigenes. The stride made in the area of motor spare parts manufacturing is unprecedented; the same applies to other parts of the eastern states. People from other neighboring African nations go to Nnewi to buy car spare parts and other commodities manufactured there. As one businessman put it: "If Nigeria ever gets into a conflict akin to the civil war, we now have viable industries in the East to somehow sustain the economy, provide employment and contribute to war efforts. We would not be caught unawares again."

Self-reliance

After the war, most Igbos began to adopt the unwritten policy of self-reliance as far as the development of their areas is concerned. No longer did they overly rely on the federal government to provide basic infrastructure like roads, pipe-borne water and electricity for them. Through self-help and communal efforts, money is raised and used to finance such projects. In the early eighties, during the first phase of electrification in Nnewi, families contributed money and procured cables, poles, transformers and meters for the installation of electricity in their neighborhoods. Also, in the mid eighties, a private citizen in my village single-handedly financed the construction of several miles of roadway for the village. This type of effort is being replicated in many other parts of the eastern states.

Someone familiar with the deplorable condition of infrastructures in the eastern states could wonder why the situation is so, if Igbos have resorted to self-reliance. The answer is simply that individuals can only do so much in a state. Also, individual effort is mainly directed at local roads and infrastructures while the federal roads are still left for the federal government to handle. Of course, the federal government has completely derelicted its duties in that regard.

Such self-help efforts, as narrated above, were rare in the eastern region before the war; Igbos mainly spent their money developing the townships where they lived throughout the North and West; they built houses, schools, churches and so on in the areas called *Sabongari* in the northern states. It was the war lesson that informed the change of attitude towards their towns.

Igbocentricity

Igbos easily adapt to any environment where they live, be it in the North or West. You would hear Igbo children, living in places like Lagos, speaking fluent Yoruba, sometimes not even able to speak their own dialect properly. Simply put, wherever the Igbos lived in Nigeria, they not only made it their home, but they adopted the ways of life of the people, wore their types of clothes, imbibed their culture, spoke their language and made friends. Two of my father's best friends when we lived in Lagos were Hausa and Yoruba: *Sajin Major* and *Pa-Bukola*. Of course *Sajin Major* betrayed him when the pogroms of 1966 started; in so doing, my father's nationalistic disposition was completely shattered. He had the opportunity to go back to Yaba College of Technology at the end of the war, but he elected to stay in the East because of the experience he had; to him, trust had become an issue. He never developed the trust he used to have for the northerners. Before we were born, he lived in the North in places like Zaria, Kano and Jos; that was after he left Okrika Grammar School. But after the war and until his passing in 1992, he never visited any of the northern states. He was one of those who believed that old habits die hard.

This was not just peculiar to my father. Even though many families went back to where they used to live in the northern and western states, some still retained some measures of distrust and animosity. Those who lived in the North still remembered that most Igbos who died in the pogrom of 1966 were betrayed by their northern Nigerian friends, and those who lived in the western states remembered that even though some of their western Nigerian friends and neighbors had not betrayed them, they had abandoned them in the heat of hostilities. All these factors have all contributed, in no small measure, to the gradual surge in what I call Igbocentricity. Igbos are now seriously questioning the fact that they are relegated to the background in Nigeria. They wonder why it is that, many years after the war, they are still sidelined in the affairs of the nation. As a majority tribe in Nigeria, they wonder why it is that, thirty-three years after the war, no Igbo person has ever risen to become the president of Nigeria. They wonder why presidents come and go in Nigeria but never make any meaningful attempt to extend development of infrastructures to the eastern states. They point to the fact that most, if not all federal roads in the eastern states are in a state of disrepair while their counterparts in the North continue to be maintained and in good condition.

The result of all this is that Igbos have now begun to agitate for a Nigerian president of Igbo extraction; they argue that if an Igbo becomes the president, chances of development being extended to the eastern states will increase.

Some Igbos have taken this further by joining in the quest for the convocation of a sovereign national conference, where all ethnic groups in Nigeria would be represented and all issues that concern their coexistence would be tabled and discussed. They feel that for them to get their fair share in the nation, for them to ensure that the burden of the civil war does not continually put them at a disadvantage vis-à-vis other Nigerians, a meeting must be held to determine how all ethnic groups should coexist and what they must get out of the union called Nigeria.

Many pan-Igbo associations are springing up in many forms all over Nigeria; the overall goal of such groups has been the empowerment of the Igbos to freely seek any elected offices they want, live wherever they want and speak their minds about any and all issues concerning Nigeria. Even in the Diaspora, these associations, like the World Igbo Congress, seem to be waxing very strong and are poised to end the marginalization of Igbos. It could be argued that with or without the civil war, these changes would have taken place anyway. I believe, however, considering how the Igbos lived in the pre-war period, that there is a very big chance that without the civil war and its attendant effects, the ethnic consciousness wave sweeping through the Igbo heartland at this time, may well not have happened. One could also argue that the civil war ended thirty-three years ago and wonder why these changes did not immediately kick in after the war. The obvious reason is that the military rulers in Nigeria would not have allowed this ethnic consciousness to endure. It became easier to actualize as a result of the advent of a semblance of true democracy in 1999.

Igbo consciousness has widened to the point where the Igbos are extraordinarily proud to wear their traditional attires to events both in Nigeria and in the Diaspora and speak their native dialect. Before the war, Igbos assimilated other cultures so much that in a gathering of Nigerians, while other ethnic groups would be proudly wearing their traditional attires and speaking their native dialects, Igbos would be wearing clothes from other cultures. It is also not a wonder that the word Igbo, which used to be anglicized as "*Ibo*," has now been changed to its correct spelling; some even insist on saying "*Ndigbo*." Again, it may be too far a stretch to attribute all these changes to the experience from the war, but I believe that the war has had something to do with them.

TIMELINE OF SELECTED EVENTS

1960
Nigeria gains independence from the British and Dr. Nnamdi Azikiwe becomes the first president while Tafawa Balewa, becomes the prime minister.

1962
Census conducted and a population of 55.6 million declared. The census figures stated that the northern states had a population of 29.8 million.

January 1966
A group of army majors of predominantly Igbo extraction, led by Major Chukwuma Nzeogwu, stages the very first coup in Nigeria. Many prominent Nigerian leaders, especially of Northern Nigerian extraction, like Sir Tafawa Balewa and Sir Ahmadu Bello, are killed. The army takes over government and Major General Johnson Thomas Umunnakwe Aguiyi Ironsi, an Igbo, becomes the first military head of state.

May 1966
Riots and violence break out in the North; Igbos are killed in large numbers by their northern Nigerian counterparts.

July 1966
Aggrieved by the coup of January 1966, and believing that it was an attempt at Igbo domination of Nigeria, a group of junior army officers, predominantly of northern Nigerian origin, stage a countercoup. Nigerian head of state, General Ironsi, is killed while on a state visit to Ibadan. He was killed along with his host, the governor of the western state, Col. Adekunle Fajuiyi.

July 1966
General Ironsi's Chief of Staff, Lt. Col. Yakubu Gowon, a northerner, emerges as the new military Head of State.

October 1966
In Northern Nigeria, soldiers and civilians rampage through the streets with machetes, spears, stones and other lethal weapons and massacre thousands of Igbos, looting and burning down their homes.

May 27, 1967
Lt. Col. Yakubu Gowon subdivides Nigeria into twelve states.

May 30, 1967
The governor of eastern region, Lt. Col. Chukwuemeka Odumegwu Ojukwu, declares an independent state for the easterners, called Biafra.

June 1967
Civil defense and militia activities begin in Biafra.

June 1967
Cameroon closes her border with Nigeria, thereby shutting any means of supplies into the eastern region.

July 6, 1967
The Biafra-Nigeria war begins.

July 29, 1967
Major Chukwuma Nzeogwu of Biafran command killed in Nsukka sector.

August 9, 1967
Biafran soldiers cross the Niger Bridge, take control of the Midwest and march as far as Ore, near Lagos.

September 20, 1967
Benin recaptured by federal troops with troops led by Col. Murtala Muhammed of Nigerian command.

September 24th 1967
Col. Victor Banjo, the officer commanding the Biafran soldiers that marched to Ore, is executed along with Lt. Col. Emmanuel Ifeajuna, Major Philip Alale and Samuel Agbam. They were charged with treason for their actions in the retreat of Biafrans from Ore and the Midwest.

October 1967
Enugu falls into the hands of federal troops and so the Biafran capital is moved to Umuahia.

October 19, 1967
Calabar falls into the hands of federal troops under the command of Lt. Col. Benjamin Adekunle and the Third Marine Commando.

March 1968
Onitsha falls into federal hands.

March 31, 1968
Biafran troops ambush and destroy a ninety-six-vehicle convoy of federal soldiers at Abagana. Federals sustain a lot of casualties and loss of equipment.

April 1968
Biafran airstrip at Obilagu captured by federal troops.

April 1968
Soldiers of the Nigerian Second Division in Onitsha, kill more than 300 Biafran civilians praying in the cathedral in Onitsha. The attack was unprovoked.

May 18 1968
Port Harcourt falls into federal hands under Col. Benjamin Adekunle.

Sept 1968
Owerri and Aba captured by the federal troops.

Sept 1968
Biafrans recapture Ikot-Ekpene.

April 22 1969
Biafra's capital city, Umuahia falls to the federal troops

April 25 1969
Biafrans recapture Owerri by routing the Sixteenth Brigade of the federal side.

January 10, 1970
General Odumegwu Ojukwu leaves Biafra for Ivory Coast.

January 12, 1970
Biafran commander General Phillip Effiong announces Biafra's surrender.

January 12, 1970
The war ends.

January 15, 1970
General Yakubu Gowon announces the formal end of the war.

APPENDIX

Some memorable speeches

L t. Col. Yakubu Gowon's first broadcast on assumption of office, after the murder of General Ironsi—August 1, 1966(courtesy Dawodu.com)

This is Lt.-Col. Y. Gowon, Army Chief of Staff, speaking to you.

My fellow countrymen, the year 1966 has certainly been a fateful year for our beloved country, Nigeria. I have been brought to the position today of having to shoulder the great responsibilities of this country and the armed forces with the consent of the majority of the members of the Supreme Military Council as a result of the unfortunate incident that occurred on the early morning of 29th July 1966.

However, before I dwell on the sad issue of 29th July 1966, I would like to recall to you the sad and unfortunate incidents of 15th January 1996, which bear relevance. According to the certain well-known facts, which have so far not been disclosed to the nation and the world, the country was plunged into a national disaster by the grave and unfortunate action taken by a section of the Army against the public. By this I mean that a group of officers, in conjunction with certain civilians, decided to overthrow the legal government of the day; but their efforts were thwarted by the inscrutable discipline and loyalty of the great majority of the Army and the other members of the armed forces and the police. The Army was called upon to take up the reins of government until such time that law and order had been restored. The attempt to overthrow the government of the day was done by eliminating political leaders and high-ranking Army officers, a majority of whom came from a particular section of the country. The Prime Minister lost his life during this uprising. But for the outstanding discipline and loyalty of the members of the Army who are most affected, and the other members of the armed forces and the police, the situation probably could have degenerated into a civil war.

There followed a period of determined effort of reconstruction ably shouldered by Maj.-Gen. J. T. U. Aguiyi-Ironsi but, unfortunately, certain parties caused suspicion and grave doubts of the Government's sincerity in several quarters. Thus, coupled with the already unpleasant experience of the 15th January still fresh in the minds of the majority of the people, certain parts of the country decided to agitate against the military regime which ad hitherto enjoyed country-wide support. It was, unfortunately, followed by serious rioting and bloodshed in many cities and towns in the North.

There followed a period of uneasy calm until the early hours of 29th July 1966, when the country was once again plunged into another very serious and grave situation, the second in seven months. The position on the early morning of 29th July was a report from Abeokuta garrison, that there was a mutiny and that two senior and one junior officer from a particular section of the country were killed. This soon spread to Ibadan and Ikeja. More casualties were reported in these places. The supreme commander was by this time at Ibadan attending the natural rulers' conference and was due to return on the afternoon of 29th July. The Government Lodge was reported attacked and the last report was that he and the West Military Governor were both kidnapped by some soldiers. Up till now, there is no confirmation of their whereabouts. The situation was soon brought under control in these places. Very shortly afterward, at about the same time, there was a report that there were similar disturbances among the troops in the North, and that a section of the troops had taken control of all military stations in the North as well. The units of Enugu and the garrison at Benin were not involved. All is now quiet and I can assure the public that I shall do all in my power to stop any further bloodshed and to restore law, order and confidence in all parts of the country with your co-operation and goodwill.

I have now come to the most difficult part, or the most important part, of this statement. I am doing it, conscious of the great disappointment and heartbreak it will cause all true and sincere lovers of Nigeria and of Nigerian unity both at home and abroad, especially our brothers in the Commonwealth.

As a result of the recent events and the other previous similar ones, I have come to strongly believe that we cannot honestly and sincerely continue in this wise, as the basis of trust and confidence in our unitary system of government has not been able to stand the test of time. I have already remarked on the issues in question. Suffice to say that, putting all considerations to test-political, economic, as well as social-the base for unity is not there or is so badly rocked, not only once but several times. I therefore feel that we should review the issue of our national standing and see if we can help stop the country form drifting away into utter destruction. With the general consensus of opinion of all the Military Governors and other members of the Supreme and Executive Council, a decree will soon be issued to lay a firm foundation of this objective. Fellow countrymen, I sincerely hope we shall be able to resolve most of the problems that have disunited us in the past and really come to respect and trust one another in accordance with an all-round code of good conduct and etiquette.

All foreigners are assured of their personal safety and should have no fear of being molested.

I intend to continue the policy laid down in the statement by the Supreme Commander on 16th January 1966 published on 26th January 1966.

We shall also honor all international treaty obligations and commitments and all financial agreements and obligations entered into by the previous government. We are desirous of maintaining good diplomatic relationships with all countries. We therefore consider any foreign interference in any form as an act of aggression.

All members of the armed forces are requested to keep within their barracks except on essential duties and when ordered from SHQ. Troops must not terrorize the public, as such action will discredit the new National Military Government. Any act of looting or sabotage will be dealt with severely. You are to remember that your task is to help restore law and order and confidence in the public in time of crisis.

I am convinced that with your co-operation and understanding, we shall be able to pull the country out of its present predicament. I promise you that I shall do all I can to return to civil rule as soon as it can be arranged. I also intend to pursue most vigorously the question of the release of political prisoners. Fellow countrymen, give me your support and I shall endeavour to live up to expectations. Thank you.

General Ojukwu's message prerecorded before he left Biafra and broadcast on Biafran radio on January 11, 1970(Dawodu.com)

Proud and heroic Biafrans, fellow countrymen and women, once again I salute you. My government has been reviewing the progress of this war that has now raged for the past two and a half years with increasing fury. It is well that at each stage we remind ourselves of the purposes of this war, what we are fighting to safeguard, and why we are so determined to continue to defend ourselves.

You have borne the brunt of the strains of this fight. You have suffered unmentionable privations at the hands of an enemy that has used every conceivable weapon, particularly the weapon of starvation, against an innocent people whose only crime is that they choose to live in peace and security according to their own beliefs and away from a country that had condemned and rejected them.

Your heroism as a people has sustained our gallant armed forces in defending the territory of our fatherland and in giving you that protection that we all so ardently need and desire. You have had your villages and homes ravaged and plundered, your assets destroyed, millions of your sons and daughters murdered in cold blood, and your youth condemned to misery by the enemy's recent movements and indiscriminate shelling and bombing of hamlets, villages, and refugees in their camps and on the roads.

All this sacrifice has been in the interest and with the sole purpose of achieving security, which was the main motive forcing our taking up arms to defend ourselves. We had proclaimed ourselves a republic, independent and sovereign, because we were and are satisfied that only through it can we guarantee our security. Nevertheless we left the door open and [declared] on several occasions that we welcomed any other initiative that would offer us the security we need. Each time we have said so our enemies and detractors have mischievously distorted our statements. We are entitled in the light of our recent experience to demand to know what measures are being proposed for our security.

The task of a leader of a people at war is to be responsive to the plight of his people, to determine what level of sacrifice can be accepted. Your patriotism has exceeded all expectations and earned worldwide admiration for your fortitude. Armed with your mandate I have striven to apply the forces at our disposal to the best of our ability against overwhelming odds. Throughout we have made strenuous efforts for peace, taking initiatives of our own to get peace talks going, made compromises in order to get our adversaries to settle our conflict at the conference table. Each time a callous world has imposed a new set of conditions. Each condition that we fulfil gives rise to an entirely new one.

More recently, some friends of both sides have made some proposals for an arrangement with Nigeria that in our view will offer to Biafrans the security to which we aspire. This has been referred to as certain forms of union, confederalties, association, or commonwealth arrangements with Nigeria.

Once more, to show our honesty, and in accord with my own frequent affirmations that I would personally go anywhere to secure peace and security for my people, I am now travelling out of Biafra to explore with our friends all these proposals further and fully and to be at hand to settle these issues to the best of my ability, always serving the interests of my people. Our detractors may see this move as a sign of collapse of our struggle, or an escape from my responsibilities.

If, God helping, we can by this latest show of earnestness secure for our people the end of destruction of your homes and property, I shall be satisfied that this venture on which I embark with your blessing has yielded fruit. I know that your prayers go with me as I go in search of peace and that, God willing, I shall soon be back among you. In my short absence I have arranged for the Chief of General Staff, Maj.-Gen. Phillip Effiong, to administer the government with the rest of the cabinet to run the affairs of this republic while I go on this mission, accompanied by my political adviser and my chief secretary.

I once more pay my tribute to the Biafra Armed Forces, and urge all ranks to maintain their positions while I seek an early and honorable end to this struggle and all the suffering it has brought on our people. Proud and courageous Biafrans, [noble] Biafrans, Biafra shall live. God bless you all.

General Yakubu Gowon announces the formal end of the war on January 15, 1970(Dawodu.com)

Citizens of Nigeria,

It is with a heart full of gratitude to God that I announce to you that today marks the formal end of the civil war. This afternoon at Dodan Barracks, Lt. Col. Phillip Effiong, Lt. Col. David Ogunewe, Lt. Col. Patrick Anwunah, Lt. Col. Patrick Amadi and Commissioner of Police, Chief Patrick Okeke formally proclaimed the end of the attempt at secession and accepted the authority of the Federal Military Government of Nigeria. They also formally accepted the present political and administrative structure of the country. This ends thirty months of a grim struggle. Thirty months of sacrifice and national agony.

Exactly four years ago on January 15, 1966, a group of young army officers overthrew the government of the country with violence. The country hoped, however, that the military regime which followed would quickly restore discipline and confidence in the army and introduce a just, honest, patriotic and progressive government. The country was disappointed in those hopes. There were further tragic incidents in the army leading to the death of many officers and men in July 1966.

I then assumed the leadership of the Federal Military Government. I gave a solemn pledge to work to reduce tension in the army and the country, to restore the federal constitution and to prepare the country for an orderly return to civilian rule as early as possible. Despite my efforts and to co-operation of all other members of the Supreme Military Council, the former Lt. Col. Ojukwu pushed us from one crisis to another. This intransigent defiance of Federal Government authority heightened tensions and led to the much regretted riots in September/October 1966. He subsequently exploited the situation to plunge the former Eastern Region into secession and the nation into a tragic war.

The world knows how hard we strove to avoid the civil war. Our objectives in fighting the war to crush Ojukwu's rebellion were always clear. We desired to preserve the territorial integrity and unity of Nigeria. For as one country we would be able to maintain lasting peace amongst our various communities; achieve rapid economic development to improve the lot of our people; guarantee a dignified future and respect in the world for our prosperity and contribute to African unity and modernization. On the other hand, the small successor states in a disintegrated Nigeria would be victims of perpetual war and misery and neo-colonialism. Our duty was clear. And we are, today, vindicated.

The so-called "Rising Sun of Biafra" is set for ever. It will be a great disservice for anyone to continue to use the word Biafra to refer to any part of the East Central State of Nigeria. The tragic chapter of violence is just ended. We are the dawn of national reconciliation. Once again, we have an opportunity to build a new nation.

My dear compatriots, we must pay homage to the fallen. To the heroes, who have made the supreme sacrifice that we may be able to build a nation great in justice, fair play, and industry. They will be mourned for ever by a grateful nation. There are also the innocent men, women, and children who perished, not in battle but as a result of the conflict. We also honor their memory. We honor the fallen of both sides of this tragic fratricidal conflict. Let it be our resolution that all those dead shall have not died in vain. Let the greater nation we shall build be their proud monument forever.

Now, my dear countrymen, we must recommence at once in greater earnest, the task of healing the nation's wounds. We have at various times repeated our desire for reconciliation in full equality, once the secessionist regime abandoned secession. I solemnly repeat our guarantees of a general amnesty for those misled into rebellion. We guarantee the security of life and property of all citizens in every part of Nigeria and equality in political rights. We also guarantee the right of every Nigerian to reside and work wherever he chooses in the Federation, as equal citizens of one united country. It is only right that we should all henceforth respect each other. We should all exercise civic restraint and use our freedom, taking into full account the legitimate right and needs of the other man. There is no question of second class citizenship in Nigeria.

On our side, we fought the war with great caution, not in anger or hatred, but always in the hope that common sense would prevail. Many times we sought a negotiated settlement, not out of weakness, but in order to minimize the problems of reintegration, reconciliation, and reconstruction. We knew that however the war ended, in the battlefield, or in the conference room, our brothers fighting under other colors must rejoin us and that we must together rebuild the nation anew.

Those now freed from the terror and misery of the secessionist enclave are therefore doubly welcome. The nation is relieved. All energies will now be bent to the task of reintegration and reconciliation. They will find, contrary to the civil [thus in press release; but probably 'evil'?] *propaganda with which they were fed, that thousands and thousands of Ibos have lived and worked in peace with other ethnic groups in Lagos and elsewhere in the Federation throughout the dark days of the civil war. There is, therefore, no cause for humiliation on the part of any group of the people of this country. The task of reconciliation is truly begun.*

The nation will be proud of the fact that the ceremony today at Dodan Barracks of reunion under the banner of the Federal Republic of Nigeria was arranged and conducted by Nigerians amongst ourselves alone. No foreign good offices were involved. That is what we always prayed for. We always prayed that we should resolve our problems ourselves, free from foreign mentors and go-betweens, however well intentioned. Thus, our nation is come of age. And the meaning of today's event must be enshrined in the nation's memory forever.

There is an urgent task to be done. The Federal Government has mounted a massive relief operation to alleviate the suffering of the people in the newly liberated areas. I have as announced, assigned special responsibility for this to a member of the Federal Executive Council. We are mobilizing adequate resources from the Federal Government to provide food, shelter, and medicines for the affected population. Rehabilitation and reconstruction will follow simultaneously to restore electricity, transport and communications. We must, as a matter of urgency, resettle firms and reopen factories to ensure that normal economic life is resumed by everyone as soon as possible. Special attention will be given to the rehabilitation of women and children in particular, so long denied the comfort of homes, the blessing of education and the assurance of a future by Ojukwu's wicked tyranny and falsehood. We must restore at once to them hope and purpose in life.

Federal troops have a special charge to give emergency relief to the people in the areas they have liberated before civilian help can come. They must continue and intensify their splendid work in this regard. The state administrations are giving emergency relief the first priority. The Rehabilitation Commissions and the Voluntary Agencies are extending their efforts. The appropriate agencies of Federal Government will soon make further announcements about additional relief measures.

My government has directed that former civil servants and public corporation officials should be promptly reinstated as they come out of hiding. Detailed arrangements for this exercise have been published. Plans for the rehabilitation of self-employed people will also be announced shortly. The problem of emergency relief is a challenge for the whole nation. We must prove ourselves equal to the task. Our resources, which have enabled us to prosecute the war successfully and without obligations to anyone, are considerable. I appeal to the nation for volunteers to help in the emergency relief operations in the newly liberated areas. Doctors, nurses, engineers, technicians, builders, plumbers, mechanics, and administrators—all skilled hands willing to help are urgently required. The detailed arrangements for recruitment will soon be announced. I am sure that there will be a prompt and good response to this call.

You will have heard that my government may seek the assistance of friendly foreign governments and bodies, especially in the provision of equipment to supplement our national effort. There are, however, a number of foreign governments and organizations whose so-called assistance will not be welcome. These are the governments and organizations which sustained the rebellion. They are thus guilty of the blood of thousands who perished because of prolongation of the futile rebel assistance. They did not act out of love for humanity. Their purpose was to disintegrate Nigeria and Africa and impose their will on us. They may still harbor their evil intentions. We shall therefore not allow them to divide and estrange us again from one another with their dubious and insulting gifts and their false humanitarianism.

Regarding the future, we shall maintain our purpose to work for stability with the existing political structure of a minimum of twelve states. The collision of three giant regions with pretentions to sovereignty created distrust and fear and to the tragic conflict now ending. The multi-state structure will therefore be retained with the minimum of the present twelve states. Immediate post-war planning and reconstruction will continue on this basis. Any new constitution will be the result of discussion by the representatives of all the people of Nigeria.

I am happy that despite the war, Nigeria has maintained a strong and expanding economy. Plans are also far advance for faster economic modernization. Our enormous material resources and our large dynamic population will make this possible. We are pledge to ensure rapid development for the benefit of the Nigerian people themselves. It will be much easier to achieve reconciliation and reintegration in increasing prosperity.

Fellow countrymen, the civil war is truly over. We thank God. But the state of national emergency and emergency regulations remain. Discipline and sacrifice are essential if we are to achieve our goals in the immediate post-war period and lay sound foundations for the future. I demand of you patience, resolution, and continued dedication. I demand of the workers and employers continued restraint in industrial relations in keeping with the recent decree. A decree on price control will soon be promulgated. We shall soon review wages and salaries to improve the lot of the ordinary man. The immediate economic problems are challenging and we must behave accordingly.

On this occasion, I wish to place on record the nation's gratitude to the Organization of African Unity for its splendid diplomatic and moral support for the Federal cause. I thank particularly the Chairman of the Consultative Committee on Nigeria, His Imperial Majesty Haile Selassie I and the other members of the committee. I also thank the President of the OAU General Assembly, Presidents Mobutu, Boumedienne, and Ahidjo, who presided over OAU summit discussions of the Nigerian crisis. The enemies of Africa were restrained by the demonstration of such solid support. I thank the Secretary General of the United Nations, U Thant, for his understanding attitude towards our country's crisis and the specialized agencies for their assistance. I also thank the friendly governments who gave us moral and material support in the darkest hour of our need. The nation will remember them as true friends. It is the desire of my government that our relations with them should grow stronger.

Consistent with our basic policy, we shall maintain correct relations with all foreign governments notwithstanding the anxieties they may have caused us. As we emerge from our greatest trial we shall endeavour to work for peace in the world and for a better economic deal for the less developed countries of the world.

The Armed Forces deserve the greatest praise for their valor in battle, their loyalty and dedication and for their resourcefulness in overcoming the formidable obstacles placed in our way. I praise them for observing strictly the code of conduct issued to them at the beginning of the operations. It is necessary now more than ever when the rebellion is ended for them to maintain the high standard they have attained. The letter and spirit of the code must be obeyed. Their first duty is to protect the lives and property of all surrendering troops and civilians and to give them humane treatment. Stern disciplinary meas-

ures will be taken against any who violate the code. I know, however, that I can continue to count on your loyalty and discipline.

I also praise the civilian population everywhere in the country for their patience, sacrifice, loyalty, and steadfast support for the fighting troops and for One Nigeria. We must all be justly proud. All Nigerians share the victory of today. The victory for national unity, victory for hopes of Africans and black people everywhere. We must thank God for his mercies. We mourn the dead heroes. We thank God for sparing us to see his glorious dawn of national reconciliation. We have ordered that Friday, Saturday, and Sunday be national days of prayer. We must his guidance to do our duty to contribute our quota to the building of a great nation, founded on the concerted efforts of all its people and on justice and equality. A nation never to return to the fractious, sterile and selfish debates that led to the tragic conflict just ending. We have overcome a lot over the past four years. I have therefore every confidence that ours will become a great nation. So help us God.

Long Live the Federal Republic of Nigeria.

0-595-26366-6

CPSIA information can be obtained
at www.ICGtesting.com
Printed in the USA
FFOW03n2111151117
43549515-42316FF